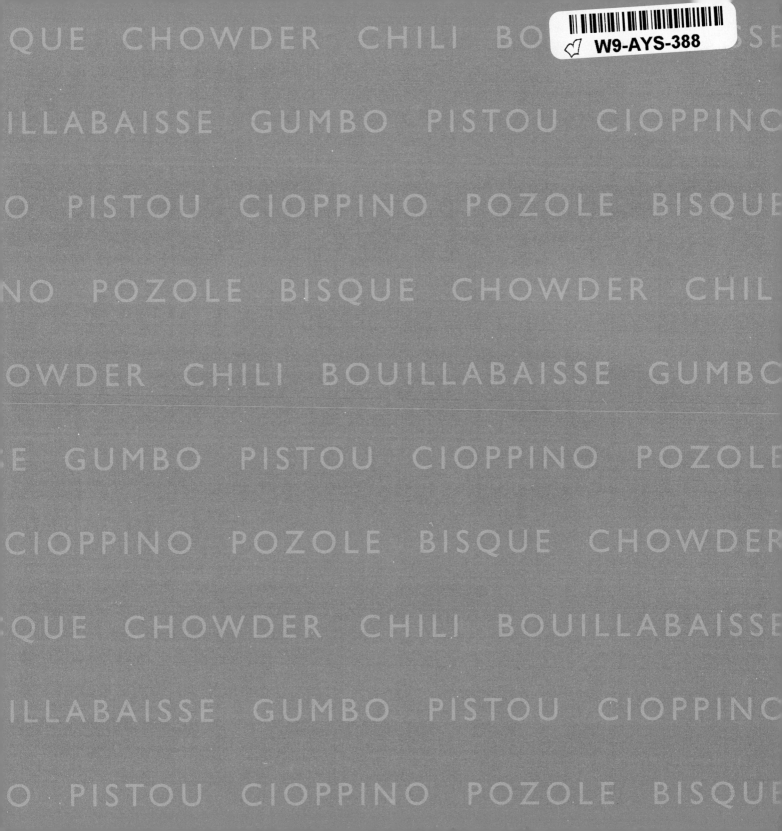

FAVORITE BRAND NAME
HEARTY
soups & stews

Publications International, Ltd.

Favorite Brand Name Recipes at www.fbnr.com

POZOLE BISQUE CHOWDER CHILI BOUILLABAISSE GUMBO PISTOU CIOPPINO

Microwave Cooking: Microwave ovens vary in wattage. Use the cooking times as guidelines and check for doneness before adding more time.

Preparation/Cooking Times: Preparation times are based on the approximate amount of time required to assemble the recipe before cooking, baking, chilling or serving. These times include preparation steps such as measuring, chopping and mixing. The fact that some preparations and cooking can be done simultaneously is taken into account. Preparation of optional ingredients and serving suggestions is not included.

Table of CONTENTS

OZOLE BISQUE CHOWDER CHILI BOUILLABAISSE GUMBO PISTOU CIOPPINO

The American Bowl

Road Trip! *Climb aboard and discover America through a variety of robust soups and comforting stews. You'll be amazed by the* **diversity.** *Just don't forget to pack your soup spoon!*

HEARTY soups & stews

4

Golden Gate Wild Rice Cioppino

2	cups chopped onions
1	medium green bell pepper, chopped
4	cloves garlic, minced
2	tablespoons olive oil
1	cup white wine
1	can (28 ounces) whole tomatoes, drained and chopped
1	bottle (8 ounces) clam juice
1	bay leaf
$\frac{1}{2}$	teaspoon dried basil leaves
$\frac{1}{2}$	teaspoon dried oregano leaves
$\frac{1}{2}$	teaspoon dried rosemary
$\frac{1}{4}$	teaspoon red pepper flakes
2	cups cooked California wild rice
6	large *or* 12 small clams, well scrubbed
$\frac{1}{2}$	pound medium shrimp, peeled and deveined
$\frac{1}{2}$	pound scallops, cut into halves crosswise
	Chopped parsley

In large stockpot or Dutch oven, sauté onions, bell pepper and garlic in oil until onion is soft. Add wine, tomatoes, clam juice, bay leaf, basil, oregano, rosemary and pepper flakes. Bring to a boil, reduce heat and simmer 30 minutes, stirring often.

Add rice and bring to a simmer. Add clams; cook until clams open. Discard any clams that do not open.

Add shrimp and scallops; cook until shrimp turn pink, about 2 to 3 minutes; do not overcook. Sprinkle with parsley.

Makes 4 servings

Favorite recipe from **California Wild Rice Advisory Board**

Golden Gate Wild Rice Cioppino

West Coast Bouillabaisse

1 cup sliced onion

2 stalks celery, cut diagonally into slices

2 cloves garlic, minced

1 tablespoon vegetable oil

4 cups chicken broth

1 can (28 ounces) tomatoes with juice, cut up

1 can (6½ ounces) minced clams with juice

½ cup dry white wine

1 teaspoon Worcestershire sauce

½ teaspoon dried thyme, crushed

¼ teaspoon bottled hot pepper sauce

1 bay leaf

1 cup frozen cooked bay shrimp, thawed

1 can (12 ounces) STARKIST® Tuna, drained and broken into chunks

Salt and pepper to taste

6 slices lemon

6 slices French bread

In Dutch oven, sauté onion, celery and garlic in oil for 3 minutes. Stir in broth, tomatoes with juice, clams with juice, wine, Worcestershire, thyme, hot pepper sauce and bay leaf. Bring to a boil; reduce heat. Simmer for 15 minutes. Stir in shrimp and tuna; cook for 2 minutes to heat. Remove bay leaf. Season with salt and pepper. Garnish with lemon slices and serve with bread.

Makes 6 servings

West Coast Bouillabaisse

1 can (5 ounces) whole baby clams, undrained

1 baking potato, peeled and coarsely chopped

¼ cup finely chopped onion

⅔ cup evaporated skim milk

¼ teaspoon white pepper

¼ teaspoon dried thyme leaves

1 tablespoon reduced-fat margarine

8

New England Clam Chowder

1. **DRAIN** juice from clams; reserve clams. Add enough water to juice to measure ⅔ cup. Combine clam juice mixture, potato and onion in large saucepan. Bring to a boil over high heat; reduce heat and simmer 8 minutes or until potato is tender.

2. **ADD** milk, pepper and thyme to saucepan. Increase heat to medium-high. Cook and stir 2 minutes. Add margarine. Cook 5 minutes or until soup thickens, stirring occasionally.

3. **ADD** clams; cook and stir 5 minutes or until clams are firm.   *Makes 2 servings*

New England Clam Chowder

1 teaspoon salt, divided

¼ teaspoon pepper

8 boneless skinless chicken thighs, cut into bite-size pieces

2 tablespoons vegetable oil

1 onion, cut lengthwise into ¼-inch slices

1 can (28 ounces) tomatoes, undrained, broken-up

2¼ cups water, divided

1 package (10 ounces) frozen lima beans

1 package (10 ounces) frozen whole kernel corn

1 tablespoon Worcestershire sauce

2 teaspoons chicken bouillon granules

1 teaspoon sugar

2 tablespoons all-purpose flour

2 tablespoons chopped parsley

Speedy Brunswick Stew

Sprinkle ¼ teaspoon salt and pepper over chicken. Heat oil in Dutch oven over medium-high heat. Add chicken and onion; cook and stir about 5 minutes.

Add tomatoes, 2 cups water, beans, corn, Worcestershire, bouillon granules, sugar and remaining ¾ teaspoon salt. Bring to a boil over high heat. Reduce heat to low. Cover and simmer 20 minutes or until chicken and vegetables are fork-tender.

Mix flour and remaining ¼ cup water in small bowl. Stir flour mixture into stew. Cook, stirring, until slightly thickened. Sprinkle with chopped parsley. *Makes 6 to 8 servings*

*Favorite recipe from **Delmarva Poultry Industry, Inc.***

*Quick*Tip

The mixture of flour and water added to this stew is called a slurry. For best results, use cold water and mix the slurry into a thin paste with no lumps. Always stir and cook soups or stews for several minutes after a slurry addition, so the flour will lose its raw taste.

Native American Wild Rice Soup

2   cups water

1/2 cup wild rice, uncooked, rinsed
     in cold water and drained

1   stick (1/2 cup) butter

1 1/2 cups onion, diced

8   ounces fresh button mushrooms,
    sliced

2   teaspoons fresh rosemary,
    stemmed, minced *or*
    3/4 teaspoon dried rosemary,
    crumbled

3/4 cup flour

8   cups chicken broth

1   teaspoon salt

1/2 teaspoon freshly ground black
     pepper

1   cup whipping cream

2   tablespoons sherry or dry white
    wine

Place water in medium saucepan. Add wild rice and bring to a boil over medium heat. Reduce heat to low, cover and simmer about 45 minutes. Do not drain; set aside. Melt butter in 5-quart Dutch oven over medium heat. Add onion and mushrooms. Sauté about 3 minutes, until vegetables soften; add rosemary. Add flour gradually to mushroom mixture, cooking and stirring frequently over medium-high heat, until mixture boils. Add chicken broth; bring to a boil. Cook 1 minute; stir in reserved wild rice and any remaining liquid, salt and pepper. Stir in whipping cream and sherry; do not boil. Serve immediately.   *Makes 12 servings*

Favorite recipe from **Wisconsin Milk Marketing Board**

*Quick*Tip

Button mushrooms are the most common mushrooms grown and sold. They are plump and dome-shaped with a smooth texture and mild flavor. To wash mushrooms, rinse under cold running water or wipe with a damp paper towel. Never scrub mushrooms as this can remove their skin.

11

HEARTY *soups & stews*

1   pound lean ground beef

1   small onion, chopped

1   can (28 ounces) crushed tomatoes with roasted garlic

1½ cups BIRDS EYE® frozen Farm Fresh Mixtures Broccoli, Cauliflower & Carrots

1   can (14½ ounces) whole new potatoes, halved

1   cup BIRDS EYE® frozen Sweet Corn

1   can (4½ ounces) chopped green chilies, drained

½   cup water

12

Texas Beef Stew

• In large saucepan, cook beef and onion over medium-high heat until beef is well browned, stirring occasionally.

• Stir in tomatoes, vegetables, potatoes with liquid, corn, chilies and water; bring to boil.

• Reduce heat to medium-low; cover and simmer 5 minutes or until heated through.   *Makes 4 servings*

Serving Suggestion: Serve over rice with warm crusty bread.

Prep Time: 5 minutes
Cook Time: 15 minutes

*Quick*Tip

The smell of onions and garlic can penetrate your cutting boards. Keep a separate cutting board exclusively for these vegetables.

Texas Beef Stew

14

1 large smoked ham hock

1 (4 to 5 pound) stewing chicken

1 small onion, sliced

1 carrot, sliced

2 ribs celery with leaves, sliced

2 teaspoons LAWRY'S® Seasoned Salt

6 tablespoons flour

1 teaspoon LAWRY'S® Seasoned Salt

1/4 teaspoon white pepper

1/4 cup butter or margarine

1/2 cup half & half

1 cup steamed, sliced carrots and green peas (optional)

Dumpling Mix

2 cups all-purpose flour

1 1/2 to 2 teaspoons LAWRY'S® Seasoned Salt

4 teaspoons baking powder

1 tablespoon shortening

3/4 cup milk

Old Virginia Chicken & Dumplings

In large soup pot, combine ham hock, chicken, onion, carrot, celery, 2 teaspoons Seasoned Salt and enough water to cover, and cook over medium-low heat until chicken is done, about 2 hours. Remove ham and chicken from stock. When cool enough to handle, remove meat from bones; dice meat and reserve. Strain stock into 1 quart measure and if needed, add more water to make 1 quart of stock. In small bowl, combine flour, 1 teaspoon Seasoned Salt and white pepper. In soup pot, heat butter over medium heat; stir in seasoned flour and cook while stirring constantly 2 to 3 minutes. Slowly add stock, stirring constantly; cook 2 minutes. Add half & half, stirring until smooth and thickened. Add diced meat and carrots and peas, if desired; adjust seasoning. Meanwhile, sift together flour, Seasoned Salt and baking powder three times. Mix in shortening with pastry blender or fork. Add milk and mix just until blended. Do not overwork dough. Dip teaspoon into cold water then into dough, spooning dough onto top of gently bubbling chicken mixture. Cook, covered, 15 minutes without lifting the lid.   *Makes 4 servings*

Baja Corn Chowder

1/4 cup butter or margarine

3 cans (17 ounces each) whole kernel corn, drained, divided

1 medium red bell pepper, diced

2 cups chicken broth

1 quart half-and-half

1 can (7 ounces) diced green chilies, drained

1 package (1.27 ounces) LAWRY'S® Spices & Seasonings for Fajitas

2 cups (8 ounces) shredded Monterey Jack cheese

1/2 teaspoon LAWRY'S® Seasoned Pepper

Hot pepper sauce to taste

In Dutch oven or large saucepan, heat butter. Add one can of corn and bell pepper and cook over medium-high heat 5 minutes, stirring occasionally. Remove from heat. In food processor or blender, place remaining two cans of corn and chicken broth; process until smooth. Add to Dutch oven with half-and-half, chilies and Spices & Seasonings for Fajitas. Return to heat. Bring just to a boil over medium-high heat, stirring constantly. Remove from heat; blend in cheese, Seasoned Pepper and hot pepper sauce.

Makes 4 to 6 servings

Serving Suggestion: Serve with warmed corn tortillas and honey butter.

15

HEARTY soups & stews

*Food*Fact

The word 'chowder' comes from the French word 'chaudière,' a stew pot French fisherman used to cook freshly caught fish. Though most commonly associated with New England clam chowder, chowders can include a variety of meats and vegetables.

Cincinnati 5-Way Chili

12 ounces ground turkey

1 cup chopped onion, divided

3 cloves garlic, minced

1 can (8 ounces) reduced-sodium tomato sauce

¾ cup water

1 to 2 tablespoons chili powder

1 tablespoon unsweetened cocoa powder

1 to 2 teaspoons cider vinegar

1 teaspoon ground cinnamon

½ teaspoon ground allspice

½ teaspoon paprika

⅛ teaspoon ground cloves (optional)

1 bay leaf

Salt and black pepper

8 ounces spaghetti, cooked and kept warm

½ cup (2 ounces) shredded fat-free Cheddar cheese

½ cup drained rinsed canned red kidney beans

1. Cook and stir turkey in medium saucepan over medium heat about 5 minutes or until browned and no longer pink. Drain excess fat. Add ½ cup onion and garlic; cook about 5 minutes or until onion is tender.

2. Add tomato sauce, water, chili powder, cocoa, vinegar, cinnamon, allspice, paprika, cloves, if desired, and bay leaf; bring to a boil. Reduce heat and simmer, covered, 15 minutes, stirring occasionally. If thicker consistency is desired, simmer uncovered, about 5 minutes more. Discard bay leaf; season to taste with salt and pepper.

3. Spoon spaghetti into bowls; spoon sauce over and sprinkle with remaining ½ cup onion, cheese and beans.

Makes 4 main-dish servings

FoodFact

Invented by Cincinnati's Greek immigrants in the early 20th century, 5-way chili recipes typically are a well-guarded family secret. The five components are the chili, a bed of thick spaghetti, warm kidney beans, fresh onions and shredded cheese.

Cincinnati 5-Way Chili

18

Nonstick cooking spray

½ pound ground sirloin or ground round beef

1 cup chopped onion

3 cups frozen mixed vegetables

1 can (14½ ounces) stewed tomatoes, undrained

2 cups water

1 cup sliced celery

1 beef bouillon cube

½ to 1 teaspoon black pepper

1 can (10½ ounces) defatted beef broth

½ cup all-purpose flour

Kansas City Steak Soup

1. Spray Dutch oven with cooking spray. Heat over medium-high heat until hot. Add beef and onion. Cook and stir 5 minutes or until beef is browned.

2. Add vegetables, tomatoes with juice, water, celery, bouillon cube and pepper. Bring to a boil. Whisk together beef broth and flour until smooth; add to beef mixture, stirring constantly. Return mixture to a boil. Reduce heat to low. Cover and simmer 15 minutes, stirring frequently.

Makes 6 servings

*Quick*Tip

If time permits, allow the soup to simmer an additional 30 minutes—the flavors just get better and better.

Easy Creole Chicken and Zucchini

Vegetable cooking spray

4 chicken quarters

1 medium onion, chopped

$^1/_4$ cup chopped green bell pepper

2 cans (14$^1/_2$ ounces each) stewed tomatoes, undrained

1 pound zucchini, chopped (about 3 medium)

$^1/_4$ cup dry sherry

1 bay leaf

1 teaspoon celery salt

$^1/_2$ teaspoon curry powder

$^1/_2$ teaspoon ground black pepper

$^1/_4$ teaspoon dried basil

4 cups hot cooked rice

Heat large Dutch oven coated with cooking spray over medium-high heat until hot. Add chicken. Cook about 10 minutes or until brown, turning occasionally. Remove chicken from pan; spoon off fat. Add onion and green pepper to pan; cook 5 minutes or until onion is tender. Stir in tomatoes and juice, zucchini, sherry, bay leaf, celery salt, curry, black pepper and basil. Arrange chicken over tomato mixture; cover and simmer over medium-low heat 30 minutes or until fork can be inserted into chicken with ease and juices run clear, not pink. Remove bay leaf. Serve over hot rice.

Makes 4 servings

Favorite recipe from **USA Rice Federation**

19

HEARTY *soups & stews*

HEARTY *soups & stews*

20

Seafood Gumbo

Cook onion, green pepper, mushrooms, and garlic in margarine in large saucepan or Dutch oven over medium-high heat until crisp-tender. Stir in tomatoes and juice, broth, red pepper, thyme, and basil. Bring to a boil. Reduce heat; simmer, uncovered, 10 to 15 minutes. Stir in okra, fish, and shrimp; simmer until fish flakes with fork, 5 to 8 minutes. Serve rice on top of gumbo. *Makes 6 servings*

Favorite recipe from **USA Rice Federation**

- $^1/_2$ cup chopped onion
- $^1/_2$ cup chopped green pepper
- $^1/_2$ cup (about 2 ounces) sliced fresh mushrooms
- 1 clove garlic, minced
- 2 tablespoons margarine
- 1 can (28 ounces) whole tomatoes, undrained
- 2 cups chicken broth
- $^1/_2$ to $^3/_4$ teaspoon ground red pepper
- $^1/_2$ teaspoon dried thyme leaves
- $^1/_2$ teaspoon dried basil leaves
- 1 package (10 ounces) frozen cut okra, thawed
- $^3/_4$ pound white fish, cut into 1-inch pieces
- $^1/_2$ pound peeled, deveined shrimp
- 3 cups hot cooked rice

GUMBO, THE MELTING POT OF STEWS, COMBINES MORE CULTURES THAN ITS MANY INGREDIENTS. THE **ROUX,** INSTILLING DARK COLOR AND RICH FLAVOR TO THIS **CREOLE** SPECIALTY, CAN BE TRACED BACK TO FRANCE. **OKRA** MADE ITS WAY TO AMERICA FROM AFRICA, WHILE MISSISSIPPI BASIN **CRAWFISH** ADD A LOCAL TOUCH. BAYOU COUNTRY DRIED **SASSAFRAS** LEAVES ARE GROUND INTO **FILÉ** POWDER, WHICH IMPARTS A WOODSY FLAVOR.

21

HEARTY soups & stews

Classic Chicken Gumbo Soup

2	tablespoons vegetable oil
2	tablespoons all-purpose flour
2	medium onions, finely chopped
1	green bell pepper, finely chopped
6	cups chicken broth
8	tomatoes, chopped
1/2	pound okra, cut into 1/4-inch pieces (2 1/2 cups)
2	ribs celery, chopped
1	teaspoon salt
1/2	teaspoon ground black pepper
1/2	teaspoon dried thyme
1	bay leaf
1	chicken, cooked, skinned, boned and cut into bite-size pieces (about 3 cups)
1	cup uncooked rice*

Recipe based on regular-milled long grain white rice. If using brown rice cook 5 to 10 minutes more.

Heat oil in large Dutch oven over low heat until hot. Add flour; stir about 15 minutes or until brown, being careful not to burn. Add onions and green pepper; cook and stir about 5 minutes or until onions are tender. Slowly add broth; stir until broth boils. Add tomatoes, okra, celery, salt, black pepper, thyme and bay leaf; bring to a boil over high heat. Add chicken and rice. Return to a boil. Reduce heat to low; cover and simmer about 20 minutes. Stir; cover and simmer 20 minutes more. Remove bay leaf. Serve immediately.

Makes 6 servings

Favorite recipe from **USA Rice Federation**

*Quick*Tip

When purchasing okra, select 2- to 3-inch pods that are deep green in color, firm and free of blemishes. You should be able to snap the pods easily and puncture them with slight pressure.

Fancy Florida Seafood Gumbo

12 ounces Florida oysters, drained

8 ounces Florida blue crab claw
      meat

½ cup chopped onion

½ cup chopped Florida celery

1 clove garlic, minced

1 tablespoon butter

1 teaspoon anise seeds

1 teaspoon salt

1 teaspoon crushed red peppers

½ teaspoon sugar

2 (20-ounce) cans diced tomatoes

1 (10-ounce) package frozen okra

Remove remaining shell or cartilage from oysters and crab and set aside. Cook onion, celery and garlic in butter until tender. Add anise, salt, peppers, sugar, tomatoes and okra. Cover and simmer for 15 minutes. Add oysters and simmer an additional 15 minutes. Add crab and heat thoroughly. Serve over rice.   *Makes 8 to 10 servings*

Favorite recipe from **Florida Department of Agriculture and Consumer Services Bureau of Seafood and Aquaculture**

23

HEARTY soups & stews

1   (6.9-ounce) package RICE-A-RONI® Chicken Flavor

1   small green bell pepper, coarsely chopped

2   tablespoons margarine or butter

1   pound boneless, skinless chicken breasts, cut into 1-inch pieces

1   (14½-ounce) can diced tomatoes with garlic and onion, undrained

¾   to 1 teaspoon Creole or Cajun seasoning

Jiffy Chicken & Rice Gumbo

1. In large skillet over medium heat, sauté rice-vermicelli mix and bell pepper with margarine until vermicelli is golden brown.

2. Slowly stir in 2¼ cups water, chicken, tomatoes, Creole seasoning and Special Seasonings; bring to a boil. Reduce heat to low. Cover; simmer 15 to 20 minutes or until rice is tender. *Makes 4 servings*

Prep Time: 5 minutes
Cook Time: 30 minutes

*Quick*Tip

To make Creole seasoning, grind ½ teaspoon cayenne pepper, ¼ teaspoon dried oregano and ¼ teaspoon dried thyme in a mortar or a clean coffee or spice grinder.

Shrimp Creole Stew

1½ cups raw small shrimp, shelled

1 bag (16 ounces) BIRDS EYE® frozen Farm Fresh Mixtures Broccoli, Cauliflower & Red Peppers

1 can (14½ ounces) diced tomatoes

1½ teaspoons salt

1 teaspoon hot pepper sauce

1 teaspoon vegetable oil

• In large saucepan, combine all ingredients.

• Cover; bring to boil. Reduce heat to medium-low; simmer 20 minutes or until shrimp turn opaque.

Makes 4 servings

Serving Suggestion: Serve over Spanish or white rice; use additional hot pepper sauce for added zip.

Prep Time: 5 minutes
Cook Time: 20 minutes

HEARTY soups & stews

26

2 tablespoons WESSON® Oil

1 cup chopped onions

½ cup sliced celery

½ cup chopped green bell pepper

2 cloves garlic, minced

2 (14½-ounce) cans chicken broth

1 (15-ounce) can HUNT'S® Tomato Sauce

1 (14½-ounce) can HUNT'S® Choice-Cut Diced Tomatoes, undrained

1½ cups cooked, chopped chicken

1 cup water

1 cup sliced fresh or frozen okra

⅓ cup uncooked rice

1 teaspoon salt

1 teaspoon hot pepper sauce

½ teaspoon thyme leaves

½ teaspoon basil leaves

½ teaspoon gumbo filé (optional)

1 bay leaf

Gumbo

In Dutch oven, heat oil; cook and stir onions, celery, bell pepper and garlic until tender. Stir in remaining ingredients. Bring to a boil; reduce heat and simmer 20 minutes. Remove bay leaf.

Makes 8 cups

*Food*Fact

Gumbo filé powder can be found in your grocer's spice aisle or gourmet section. As with most spices, filé can be stored in a cool, dark place for up to 6 months.

New Orleans Stew

2 green bell peppers, chopped

1 onion, chopped

3 ribs celery, chopped

2 tablespoons seafood seasoning

1 tablespoon dried marjoram leaves

Salt and black pepper to taste

1 pound HILLSHIRE FARM® Hot Links, sliced

4 ears corn on the cob, cut into quarters

1 pound unpeeled raw shrimp

Seafood cocktail sauce

Place bell peppers, onion and celery into large saucepan or Dutch oven; cover with water. Add seafood seasoning, marjoram, salt and black pepper to saucepan. Boil 10 to 15 minutes. Add Hot Links and corn to saucepan; boil 5 to 10 minutes. Add shrimp; boil 3 minutes. Remove pan from heat; let stand 5 minutes. Drain in colander. Serve with cocktail sauce.

Makes 8 servings

27

*Quick*Tip

Marjoram is an herb with oval, pale green leaves and a sweet, mild flavor similar to that of oregano. Dried marjoram leaves can be found in the spice aisles of most supermarkets.

HEARTY soups & stews

Shrimp Étouffée

3	tablespoons vegetable oil
¼	cup all-purpose flour
1	cup chopped onion
1	cup chopped green bell pepper
½	cup chopped carrots
½	cup chopped celery
4	cloves garlic, minced
1	can (14½ ounces) clear vegetable broth
1	bottle (8 ounces) clam juice
½	teaspoon salt
2½	pounds large shrimp, peeled and deveined
1	teaspoon crushed red pepper
1	teaspoon hot pepper sauce
4	cups hot cooked white or basmati rice
½	cup chopped flat leaf parsley

1. Heat oil in Dutch oven over medium heat. Add flour; cook and stir 10 to 15 minutes or until flour mixture is deep golden brown. Add onion, bell pepper, carrots, celery and garlic; cook and stir 5 minutes.

2. Stir in broth, clam juice and salt; bring to a boil. Simmer, uncovered, 10 minutes or until vegetables are tender. Stir in shrimp, red pepper and pepper sauce; simmer 6 to 8 minutes or until shrimp are opaque.

3. Ladle into eight shallow bowls; top each with ½ cup rice. Sprinkle with parsley. Serve with additional hot pepper sauce, if desired.

Makes 8 servings

Shrimp Étouffée

Southwestern Beef Stew

¼ cup all-purpose flour

1 teaspoon salt

1 teaspoon chili powder

1 teaspoon ground cumin

1 pound lean beef stew meat*, cut into 1-inch cubes

2 teaspoons vegetable oil

1 large onion, cut into chunks

2 teaspoons fresh or bottled minced garlic

1 can (about 14 ounces) reduced-sodium beef broth

½ cup prepared salsa or picante sauce

12 ounces red potatoes, cut into 1-inch chunks

1 cup (4 ounces) baby carrots

2 green or yellow bell peppers (or 1 of each), cut into 1-inch chunks

¼ cup chopped fresh cilantro

If lean stew meat is not available, choose lean top round steak or chuck steak; trim and cut into cubes.

1. Place flour and seasonings in large resealable plastic food storage bag. Add beef; shake to coat. Heat oil in large deep nonstick skillet or Dutch oven over medium heat until hot. Remove beef from bag; reserve remaining flour mixture. Add beef to skillet; brown on all sides, about 5 minutes. Remove and set aside.

2. Add onion and garlic to same skillet. Cook 5 minutes over medium heat, stirring occasionally. Sprinkle reserved flour mixture over onion mixture; cook and stir 1 minute. Add beef broth and salsa; bring to a boil. Return beef and any accumulated juices to skillet. Reduce heat; cover and simmer over low heat 40 minutes.

3. Stir in potatoes, carrots and bell peppers. Cover; simmer 35 to 40 minutes or until beef and vegetables are tender. Sprinkle with cilantro. *Makes 6 (1¼-cup) servings*

Note: Substitute 1 tablespoon Mexican seasoning for mixture of salt, chili powder and cumin, if desired.

Serving Suggestion: Cornbread is the perfect side to this flavorful stew.

Prep Time: 20 minutes
Cook Time: 1 hour 20 minutes

Southwestern Beef Stew

32

4 strips uncooked bacon, chopped

1 large onion, chopped

2 cloves garlic, minced

2 cans (15 ounces each) black-eye peas, undrained

1 can (14½ ounces) reduced-sodium chicken broth

3 to 4 tablespoons *Frank's® RedHot®* Cayenne Pepper Sauce

1 teaspoon dried thyme leaves

1 bay leaf

2 cups cooked long grain rice (¾ cup uncooked rice)

2 tablespoons minced fresh parsley

Hoppin' John Soup

1. Cook bacon, onion and garlic in large saucepan over medium-high heat 5 minutes or until vegetables are tender.

2. Add peas with liquid, broth, ½ cup water, **Frank's RedHot** Sauce, thyme and bay leaf. Bring to a boil. Reduce heat to low; cook, covered, 15 minutes, stirring occasionally. Remove and discard bay leaf.

3. Combine rice and parsley in medium bowl. Spoon rice evenly into 6 serving bowls. Ladle soup over rice.

Makes 6 servings

Note: For an attractive presentation, pack rice mixture into small ramekin dishes. Unmold into soup bowls. Ladle soup around rice.

Prep Time: 15 minutes
Cook Time: 20 minutes

*Food*Fact

Hoppin' John is traditionally eaten in the South on New Year's Day for good luck, but Yankees and the less superstitious can enjoy this soup any day of the year.

Hoppin' John Soup

HEARTY soups & stews

Fiesta Soup

6 boneless, skinless chicken tenderloins, cut into 1-inch pieces

2 cans (14½ ounces) low-sodium chicken broth

1 can (15 ounces) kidney beans, undrained

1 cup salsa

1 cup frozen corn

½ cup UNCLE BEN'S® Instant Rice

⅓ cup shredded Monterey Jack cheese

1. In large saucepan, combine chicken, broth, kidney beans, salsa and corn.

2. Bring to a boil. Reduce heat and simmer uncovered 5 to 10 minutes or until chicken is no longer pink. Stir in rice. Cover; remove from heat and let stand covered 5 minutes. Top each serving with cheese. *Makes 4 servings*

*Quick*Tip

Garnish with tortilla chips, sliced avocado or toasted tortilla strips.

Arizona Stew

3 tablespoons olive oil

5 medium carrots, cut into thick slices

1 large onion, wedged

1 pound sliced turkey breast, cut into 1-inch strips

1 teaspoon LAWRY'S® Garlic Powder with Parsley

3 tablespoons all-purpose flour

8 small red potatoes, cut into 1/2-inch cubes

1 package (1.48 ounces) LAWRY'S® Spices & Seasonings for Chili

1 package (10 ounces) frozen peas, thawed

8 ounces sliced fresh mushrooms

1 cup beef broth

1 can (8 ounces) tomato sauce

In large skillet, heat oil. Add carrots and onion and cook over medium-high heat until tender. Stir in turkey strips and Garlic Powder with Parsley; cook 3 minutes until turkey is just browned. Stir in flour. Pour mixture into a 3-quart casserole dish. Stir in remaining ingredients. Cover and bake in 450°F oven 45 to 50 minutes. Let stand 5 minutes before serving.

Makes 8 to 10 servings

Stove Top Directions: Prepare as above in Dutch oven. Bring mixture to a boil over medium-high heat; reduce heat to low, cover and simmer, 40 to 45 minutes until potatoes are tender. Let stand 5 minutes.

Serving Suggestion: Perfect with a crisp green salad.

Hint: Dollop top of casserole with prepared dumpling mix during the last 15 minutes of baking.

36

1 tablespoon vegetable oil

1½ pounds beef stew meat, cut into bite-size pieces

1 can (28 ounces) stewed tomatoes, undrained

2 medium carrots, cut into ¼-inch slices

1 medium onion, coarsely chopped

2 tablespoons diced green chilies

1 package (1.0 ounce) LAWRY'S® Taco Spices & Seasonings

½ teaspoon LAWRY'S® Seasoned Salt

¼ cup water

2 tablespoons all-purpose flour

1 can (15 ounces) pinto beans, drained

Santa Fe Stew Olé

In Dutch oven, heat oil. Brown stew meat over medium-high heat. Add tomatoes, carrots, onion, green chilies, Taco Spices & Seasonings and Seasoned Salt; mix well. Bring to a boil over medium-high heat; reduce heat to low and cook, covered, 40 minutes. In small bowl, combine water and flour; mix well. Stir into stew mixture. Add pinto beans; cook over low heat 15 minutes. *Makes 4 servings*

Serving Suggestion: Serve with warm corn and flour tortillas.

Santa Fe Stew Olé

½ pound lean ground pork

½ cup chopped onion

4 cups canned crushed tomatoes

2 cups chicken broth

1 (8-ounce) jar salsa, medium or hot

1 teaspoon ground cumin

1 teaspoon chili powder

½ teaspoon salt

½ teaspoon garlic powder

½ teaspoon ground black pepper

4 corn tortillas, cut into thin strips

Spicy Tortilla Soup

Brown pork and onion over medium-high heat in large saucepan, stirring occasionally. Add remaining ingredients except tortilla strips. Cover and simmer 20 minutes. Stir tortilla strips into soup and simmer 5 to 10 minutes more, until tortilla strips are softened. Serve hot.

Makes 6 servings

Prep Time: 10 minutes
Cook Time: 20 minutes

Favorite recipe from **National Pork Board**

*Quick*Tip

To preserve the quality and freshness of dried spices and herbs, buy them in small quantities and keep them for no more than 6 months. All spices and herbs should be stored tightly covered and away from heat and light.

Southwest Lamb Barley Soup

1 tablespoon vegetable oil

¾ pound fresh American lamb
  shoulder, cut into ½-inch
  cubes

½ cup chopped green onions,
  including tops

2 cloves garlic, minced

4 cups water

1 can (14½ ounces) Mexican-style
  tomatoes and juice, broken
  up, undrained

⅓ cup quick cooking barley

1 tablespoon chicken bouillon
  granules

½ teaspoon ground cumin

3 dashes hot pepper sauce

2 cups frozen corn *or* 1 can
  (16 ounces) drained whole
  kernel corn

2 tablespoons chopped fresh
  parsley or cilantro

  Coarsely crushed corn chips for
  topping (optional)

In 4-quart saucepan, heat oil and sauté lamb, onions and garlic until lamb is no longer pink.

Add water, tomatoes with juice, barley, bouillon, cumin and pepper sauce. Simmer 15 minutes.

Stir in corn; simmer 10 minutes. Stir in parsley and serve. Top each serving with crushed corn chips, if desired.

Makes 8 servings

Slow Cooker Directions: Combine all ingredients, except parsley and corn chips; place in slow cooker on LOW for 4 to 6 hours.

Prep Time: 10 minutes
Cook Time: 30 minutes

*Favorite recipe from **American Lamb Council***

39

HEARTY *soups & stews*

Idaho Potato Gazpacho

2 teaspoons olive oil

2 tablespoons minced garlic

2 medium onions, chopped

4 medium Idaho Potatoes, well scrubbed and diced

1 cup water

10 plum tomatoes, washed, halved crosswise and seeded

1 red or yellow bell pepper, washed, seeded and chopped

1 large cucumber, peeled and seeded

4 cups tomato juice

Salt and black pepper to taste

1/2 cup chopped fresh dill

Juice of 1 lemon

Dill sprigs for garnish

1. Heat olive oil in large heavy stockpot over high heat. Add garlic and stir about 30 seconds. Add onions and stir 2 minutes, until onions are tender. Reduce heat to medium; add potatoes and water. Stir and cover. Cook 8 minutes or until potatoes are tender. Cool.

2. Meanwhile, finely chop tomatoes, pepper and cucumber in food processor, working in small batches. Add vegetables to stockpot with potatoes, stirring to scrape up all browned bits. Add tomato juice, salt and pepper to taste and fresh dill. Stir to combine.

3. Chill soup in refrigerator. Just before serving, add lemon juice and stir. Serve cold, with dill sprigs for garnish, if desired.

Makes 10 (1-cup) servings

Favorite recipe from **Idaho Potato Commission**

Home-Style Chicken and Sweet Potato Stew

4 boneless, skinless chicken breasts

Garlic salt and pepper

1/2 cup all-purpose flour

1/4 cup WESSON® Vegetable Oil

2 cups cubed, peeled sweet potatoes

1 cup chopped onion

1 (14.5-ounce) can HUNT'S® Stewed Tomatoes, lightly crushed

3/4 cup homemade chicken stock or canned chicken broth

3/4 cup apple cider

1/2 teaspoon dried dill weed

1 chicken bouillon cube

Dash or two of GEBHARDT® Hot Pepper Sauce

Salt to taste

Rinse chicken and pat dry; cut into 1/2-inch pieces. Sprinkle with garlic salt and pepper. Place flour in plastic bag. Add chicken; shake until chicken is well coated. In large stockpot, heat Wesson Oil. Add chicken; cook on both sides until golden brown. Remove chicken; set aside. In same pot, add sweet potatoes and onion; sauté until onion is tender. Stir in *remaining* ingredients *except* salt; blend well. Add browned chicken; bring to a boil. Reduce heat; cover and simmer 25 to 30 minutes or until chicken is no longer pink in center and potatoes are tender, stirring often. Salt to taste.

Makes 4 servings

Tip: For a sweeter stew, substitute yams for sweet potatoes.

41

HEARTY *soups & stews*

New Mexican Pork Pozole

1	cup uncooked dried lima beans, rinsed
2	tablespoons vegetable oil
1	pound pork tenderloin, cut into 1-inch cubes
1½	cups chopped onions
3	cloves garlic, minced
2	cups canned chicken broth
1	can (14½ ounces) whole tomatoes, undrained, chopped
2	bay leaves
1	teaspoon ground cumin
1	teaspoon ground coriander
½	teaspoon crushed red pepper
1	can (16 ounces) yellow hominy, drained
3	medium zucchini, diced
	Hot cooked brown rice

1. **PLACE** beans in medium saucepan and cover with 4 inches of water. Bring to a boil over high heat; boil 2 minutes. Remove from heat. Cover and let soak 1 hour.

2. **HEAT** oil in Dutch oven over medium-high heat. Add pork; cook until browned, stirring frequently. Remove pork with slotted spoon; set aside.

3. **ADD** onions and garlic to Dutch oven; cook and stir 3 minutes or until onions are tender. Remove from heat.

4. **DRAIN** beans; add to onion mixture. Add pork, chicken broth, tomatoes with juice, bay leaves, cumin, coriander and crushed red pepper. Bring to a boil over high heat. Reduce heat to low; simmer, partially covered, 1½ hours.

5. **ADD** hominy and zucchini to bean mixture; simmer, covered, 25 to 30 minutes or until beans are tender. Remove bay leaves; discard.

6. **SPOON** hot rice into serving bowls. Top with pozole. Garnish with fresh cilantro and habañero pepper, if desired.

Makes 6 to 8 servings

New Mexican Pork Pozole

Santa Fe Taco Stew

1 tablespoon vegetable oil

1/2 cup diced onion

1/2 teaspoon LAWRY'S® Garlic
   Powder with Parsley

1 package (1.0 ounce) LAWRY'S®
   Taco Spices & Seasonings

1 can (28 ounces) diced tomatoes,
   undrained

1 can (15 ounces) pinto beans,
   drained

1 can (8¾ ounces) whole kernel
   corn, drained

1 can (4 ounces) diced green
   chilies, drained

1 cup beef broth

1/2 teaspoon cornstarch

1 pound pork butt or beef chuck,
   cooked and shredded

   Dairy sour cream (garnish)

   Tortilla chips (garnish)

   Fresh cilantro (garnish)

In Dutch oven or large saucepan, heat oil. Add onion and Garlic Powder with Parsley and cook over medium-high heat 2 to 3 minutes until onion is tender. Add Taco Spices & Seasonings, tomatoes, beans, corn and chilies; mix well. In small bowl, gradually combine broth and cornstarch, using wire whisk. Stir into stew. Add cooked meat. Bring to a boil over medium-high heat, stirring frequently. Reduce heat to low; cook, uncovered, 30 minutes, stirring occasionally. (Or, cook over low heat longer for a thicker stew.)

Makes 8 servings

Serving Suggestion: Garnish each serving with sour cream, tortilla chips and fresh cilantro, if desired.

Hint: Substitute 3 cups cooked, shredded chicken for pork or beef.

Santa Fe Taco Stew

Southwestern Chicken Soup

½ teaspoon salt

¼ teaspoon black pepper

¼ teaspoon garlic powder

1 tablespoon olive oil

1 pound boneless skinless chicken breast halves

1 medium onion, halved and sliced

1 small hot chili pepper, seeded and chopped (optional)

4 cans (about 14 ounces each) fat-free reduced-sodium chicken broth

2 cups peeled and diced potatoes

2 small zucchini, sliced

1½ cups frozen corn

1 cup diced tomato

1 tablespoon chopped fresh cilantro

2 tablespoons lime or lemon juice

1. Combine salt, black pepper and garlic powder in small bowl; sprinkle evenly over chicken.

2. Heat oil in Dutch oven over medium-high heat. Add chicken; cook, without stirring, 2 minutes or until golden. Turn chicken and cook 2 minutes more. Add onion and chili pepper, if desired. Cook 2 minutes longer, adding a little chicken broth if needed to prevent burning.

3. Add chicken broth; bring to a boil. Stir in potatoes. Reduce heat to a simmer; cook 5 minutes. Add zucchini, corn and tomato; cook 10 minutes longer or until vegetables are tender. Just before serving, stir in cilantro and lime juice.

Makes 6 servings

Prep Time: 10 minutes
Cook Time: 22 minutes

Quick **Tip**

Hot chili peppers can sting and irritate the skin; wear rubber gloves when handling peppers and do not touch your eyes. Wash your hands after handling.

Southwestern Chicken Soup

3   dried ancho chilies (each about 4 inches long) *or* 6 dried New Mexico chilies (each about 6 inches long)

2   small zucchini

1   medium onion, thinly sliced

3   cloves garlic, minced

1   teaspoon ground cumin

3   cans (about 14 ounces each) fat-free reduced-sodium chicken broth

$1\frac{1}{2}$ to 2 cups (8 to 12 ounces) shredded cooked dark turkey meat

1   can (15 ounces) chick-peas or black beans, rinsed and drained

1   package (10 ounces) frozen corn

$\frac{1}{4}$ cup cornmeal

1   teaspoon dried oregano leaves

$\frac{1}{3}$ cup chopped fresh cilantro

Southwest Corn and Turkey Soup

1. Cut stems from chilies; shake out seeds. Place chilies in medium bowl; cover with boiling water. Let stand 20 to 40 minutes or until chilies are soft; drain. Cut open lengthwise and lay flat on work surface. With edge of small knife, scrape chili pulp from skin. Finely mince pulp; set aside.

2. Cut zucchini in half lengthwise; slice crosswise into $\frac{1}{2}$-inch-wide pieces. Set aside.

3. Spray large saucepan with cooking spray; heat over medium heat. Add onion; cook, covered, 3 to 4 minutes or until light golden brown, stirring several times. Add garlic and cumin; cook and stir about 30 seconds or until fragrant. Add chicken broth, reserved chili pulp, zucchini, turkey, chick-peas, corn, cornmeal and oregano; bring to a boil over high heat. Reduce heat to low; simmer 15 minutes or until zucchini is tender. Stir in cilantro; ladle into bowls and serve.

Makes 6 servings

*Quick*Tip

Thicker-skinned ancho chilies will yield more flesh than thinner-skinned New Mexico chilies. Ancho chilies are the dried form of poblano chilies.

Country Chicken Stew

6 slices bacon, diced

2 leeks, chopped (white part only) (about ½ pound)

3 shallots, chopped

1 medium carrot, cut into ¼-inch pieces

1½ pounds boneless skinless chicken thighs, cut into 1-inch pieces

1½ pounds boneless skinless chicken breasts, cut into 1-inch pieces

½ pound boneless smoked pork butt, cut into 1-inch pieces

1 Granny Smith apple, cored and diced

2 cups dry white wine or chicken broth

1½ teaspoons herbes de Provence, crushed*

1 teaspoon salt

Pepper to taste

2 bay leaves

2 cans (15 ounces each) cannellini beans or Great Northern beans, drained

*Substitute ¼ teaspoon each rubbed sage, crushed dried rosemary, thyme, oregano, marjoram and basil leaves for herbes de Provence.

Cook and stir bacon in 5-quart Dutch oven over medium-high heat until crisp. Add leeks, shallots and carrot; cook and stir vegetables until leeks and shallots are soft. Stir in chicken, pork, apple, wine and seasonings. Bring to a boil over high heat. Reduce heat to low. Cover and simmer 30 minutes.

Stir in beans. Cover and simmer 25 to 30 minutes more or until chicken and pork are fork-tender and no longer pink in center. Remove bay leaves before serving.

Makes 8 to 10 servings

QuickTip

Choose leeks that are no more than 1½ inches in diameter. Larger leeks are not as tender or flavorful.

49

HEARTY *soups & stews*

This Hearty World

*You don't have to travel the world for a **global tour** of soups and stews. Simply choose your favorite hearty bowlful from the many **exotic locales,** including Ireland, Cuba, Vietnam and Northern Africa. So get your culinary passport in order and enjoy!*

1 tablespoon olive oil

1 medium onion, coarsely chopped

1½ pounds fresh lean American lamb boneless shoulder, cut into ¾-inch cubes

1 bottle (12 ounces) beer *or* ¾ cup water

1 teaspoon seasoned pepper

2 cans (14½ ounces each) beef broth

1 package (.93 ounces) brown gravy mix

3 cups cubed potatoes

2 cups thinly sliced carrots

2 cups shredded green cabbage

⅓ cup chopped fresh parsley (optional)

Patrick's Irish Lamb Soup

In 3-quart saucepan with cover, heat oil. Add onion and sauté until brown, stirring occasionally. Add lamb and sauté, stirring until browned. Stir in beer and pepper. Cover and simmer 30 minutes.

Mix in broth and gravy mix. Add potatoes and carrots; cover and simmer 15 to 20 minutes or until vegetables are tender. Stir in cabbage and cook just until cabbage turns bright green. Serve. Garnish with chopped parsley, if desired.

Makes 8 servings

*Favorite recipe from **American Lamb Council***

Patrick's Irish Lamb Soup

1   package (16 ounces) frozen
    vegetable medley, such as
    broccoli, cauliflower, sugar
    snap peas and red bell peppers

1   can (about 14 ounces) vegetable
    broth

¾   cup uncooked instant brown rice

2   teaspoons curry powder

½   teaspoon salt

½   teaspoon hot pepper sauce

1   can (14 ounces) unsweetened
    coconut milk

1   tablespoon fresh lime juice

Curried Vegetable-Rice Soup

1. Combine vegetables and broth in large saucepan. Cover; bring to a boil over high heat. Stir in rice, curry powder, salt and pepper sauce to taste; reduce heat to medium-low. Cover and simmer 8 minutes or until rice is tender, stirring once.

2. Stir in coconut milk; cook 3 minutes or until heated through. Remove from heat. Stir in lime juice. Ladle into shallow bowls and serve immediately.   *Makes 4 servings*

Prep and Cook Time: 16 minutes

Quick Tip

For a lighter soup with less fat and calories, substitute light unsweetened coconut milk, carried in most large supermarkets in the international foods section.

Curried Vegetable-Rice Soup

Three-Bean Caribbean Chili

1 tablespoon olive oil

1 large onion, chopped

2 cloves garlic, minced

1 jalapeño pepper,* seeded and minced

2 large red or green bell peppers, diced

1 tablespoon plus 2 teaspoons sweet paprika

1 tablespoon plus 2 teaspoons chili powder

2 teaspoons sugar

2 teaspoons ground cumin

½ teaspoon salt

¼ teaspoon ground cloves

1 can (6 ounces) tomato paste

3 cups water

1 can (15 ounces) red kidney beans, drained

1 can (15 ounces) cannellini beans, drained

1 can (15 ounces) black beans, drained

1 tablespoon balsamic vinegar

Mango Salsa (recipe follows)

Hot cooked brown rice

Fresh cilantro for garnish

Jalapeño peppers can sting and irritate the skin; wear rubber gloves when handling peppers and do not touch eyes. Wash hands after handling.

1. Heat oil in large saucepan over medium heat until hot. Add onion and garlic; cook and stir 4 minutes. Add jalapeño and bell peppers; cook and stir 5 minutes or until tender.

2. Add paprika, chili powder, sugar, cumin, salt and cloves; cook and stir 1 minute.

3. Stir in tomato paste and water until blended. Bring to a boil over high heat. Reduce heat to low. Cover and simmer 15 minutes. Stir in beans and vinegar; partially cover and simmer 15 minutes or until hot.

4. Meanwhile, prepare Mango Salsa.

5. Serve chili over rice. Top with Mango Salsa. Garnish, if desired. *Makes 6 (1-cup) servings*

Mango Salsa

1 large mango, peeled and cut into ¾-inch cubes

1 small, firm, ripe banana, peeled and cubed

3 tablespoons minced fresh cilantro

1 tablespoon thawed frozen orange juice concentrate

1 teaspoon balsamic vinegar

Combine mango, banana and cilantro in medium bowl. Stir together juice concentrate and vinegar. Pour over fruit; toss.
Makes 1¼ cups

Three-Bean Caribbean Chili

Catalonian Stew

2 boneless skinless chicken breasts, cut into bite-size pieces

3 ounces pepperoni, diced

1 tablespoon vegetable oil

2 cans (15 ounces each) tomato sauce

3 cups chicken broth

1 cup pimiento-stuffed olives, halved

2 tablespoons sugar

8 ounces uncooked rotini or other shaped pasta

$1/3$ cup chopped parsley

$1/8$ teaspoon crushed saffron, optional

1 cup (4 ounces) SARGENTO® Fancy Mild or Sharp Cheddar Shredded Cheese

1 cup (4 ounces) SARGENTO® Fancy Monterey Jack Shredded Cheese

In Dutch oven, cook chicken and pepperoni in oil over medium heat until chicken is lightly browned, about 5 minutes; drain. Add tomato sauce, chicken broth, olives and sugar. Bring to a boil; reduce heat and simmer, covered, 15 minutes. Return to a boil. Add rotini, parsley and saffron, if desired; cover and cook an additional 15 minutes or until pasta is tender. Combine Cheddar and Monterey Jack cheeses in small bowl. Spoon stew into 6 individual ovenproof serving bowls; sprinkle evenly with cheese. Bake in preheated 350°F oven about 5 minutes or until cheese is melted.

Makes 6 servings

Burgundy Beef Stew

¾ pound beef sirloin steak, cut into 1-inch cubes

1 cup diagonally sliced carrots

¼ cup Burgundy or other dry red wine

1 teaspoon minced garlic

2⅓ cups canned beef broth

1 can (14½ ounces) diced tomatoes, undrained

1 box UNCLE BEN'S® COUNTRY INN® Rice Pilaf

1 jar (15 ounces) whole pearl onions, drained

1. Generously spray large saucepan or Dutch oven with nonstick cooking spray. Heat over high heat until hot. Add beef; cook 2 to 3 minutes or until no longer pink. Stir in carrots, wine and garlic; cook 2 minutes.

2. Add broth, tomatoes with juice, rice and contents of seasoning packet. Bring to a boil. Cover; reduce heat and simmer 10 minutes, stirring occasionally. Add onions; cook 10 minutes more or until rice is tender. Remove from heat and let stand, covered, 5 minutes.   *Makes 4 servings*

Variation: One 15-ounce can of drained sweet peas and pearl onions can be substituted for the pearl onions.

57

HEARTY soups & stews

OZOLE BISQUE CHOWDER CHILI BOUILLABAISSE GUMBO PISTOU CIOPPINO

Pierogy Wonton Soup

In large saucepan, heat oil over medium-high heat. Add bok choy, carrots, garlic and ginger; cook and stir constantly until bok choy is barely tender, about 1 minute. Add broth and soy sauce; bring to a boil. Add pierogies and cook until heated through, about 5 to 7 minutes. Stir in radishes. Sprinkle with sesame seeds, if desired.

Makes 6 cups

1   tablespoon peanut or vegetable oil

2½   cups bok choy cabbage,* cut into ½-inch pieces

½   cup carrots, cut into matchsticks**

1   teaspoon minced garlic

½   teaspoon ground ginger

2   cans (about 15 ounces each) ready-to-serve chicken broth

1   teaspoon soy sauce

1   package (16.9 ounces) MRS. T'S® Frozen Potato And Cheddar Cheese or Potato And Onion Pierogies

¼   cup sliced radishes

     Sesame seeds (optional)

*If bok choy cabbage is not available, use fresh spinach, adding just before pierogies are cooked through.

**For carrot matchsticks, cut carrot into thin diagonal slices; stack 3 or 4 slices and cut into narrow sticks.

HEARTY soups & stews

58

Quick Tip

Bok choy is a popular ingredient in Asian cuisines. It is also sometimes referred to as Chinese chard, pak choi, white mustard cabbage or Chinese mustard. Look for bunches that have firm, white stalks and crisp, dark-green leaves.

Pierogy Wonton Soup

2   tablespoons olive oil, divided

4   lamb shanks (about 1 pound
    each)

2   large onions, chopped

5   cloves garlic, minced and divided

1   can (28 ounces) Italian-style
    plum tomatoes, undrained
    and coarsely chopped

½   cup dry vermouth

1½ teaspoons dried basil leaves,
    crushed

1½ teaspoons dried rosemary,
    crushed

1   teaspoon salt

½   teaspoon black pepper

1   can (19 ounces) cannellini
    beans, rinsed and drained

1½ tablespoons balsamic vinegar
    (optional)

2   tablespoons chopped fresh
    Italian parsley

1   teaspoon grated lemon peel

    Fresh lovage leaves and lemon
    peel twists for garnish

Provençal-Style Lamb Shanks

1. Heat 1 tablespoon oil in Dutch oven over medium heat until hot. Add 2 lamb shanks. Brown on all sides; transfer to large plate with tongs. Repeat with remaining 1 tablespoon oil and 2 lamb shanks.

2. Add onions and 4 cloves garlic to drippings in Dutch oven; cook 6 to 8 minutes until onions are tender, stirring occasionally.

3. Add tomatoes with juice, vermouth, basil, rosemary, salt and pepper; bring to a boil over medium-high heat. Return shanks to Dutch oven. Reduce heat to low; cover and simmer 1½ hours or until shanks are tender.

4. Remove shanks; cool slightly. Skim fat from pan juices with large spoon; discard.

5. Stir beans into pan juices; heat through. Cut lamb from shanks into 1-inch pieces with utility knife; discard bones and gristle. Return lamb to Dutch oven; heat through. Stir in vinegar.

6. Combine parsley, lemon peel and remaining clove garlic in small bowl. To serve, ladle lamb mixture into 6 individual shallow serving bowls; sprinkle with parsley mixture. Garnish, if desired.

Makes 6 servings (about 10 cups)

North African Chicken Soup

$\frac{1}{2}$	teaspoon paprika
$\frac{1}{4}$	teaspoon ground cumin
$\frac{1}{4}$	teaspoon ground ginger
$\frac{1}{4}$	teaspoon ground allspice
4	ounces boneless skinless chicken breast, cut into bite-size pieces
	Nonstick olive oil cooking spray
$1\frac{1}{4}$	cups fat-free, reduced-sodium chicken broth
1	cup peeled sweet potato cut into $\frac{1}{2}$-inch pieces
$\frac{1}{2}$	cup chopped onion
$\frac{1}{4}$	cup water
2	cloves garlic, minced
$\frac{1}{2}$	teaspoon sugar
1	cup undrained canned tomatoes, cut up
	Black pepper

1. Combine paprika, cumin, ginger and allspice. Toss $\frac{1}{2}$ teaspoon spice mixture with chicken pieces.

2. Spray medium saucepan with cooking spray. Heat over medium-high heat. Add chicken. Cook and stir 2 to 3 minutes or until chicken is no longer pink. Remove from saucepan.

3. In same saucepan combine broth, sweet potato, onion, water, garlic, sugar and remaining spice mixture. Bring to a boil. Reduce heat and simmer, covered, 10 minutes or until sweet potato is tender. Stir in tomatoes and chicken. Heat through. Season to taste with pepper.   *Makes 2 servings*

61

HEARTY soups & stews

62

Moroccan Pork Tagine

1 pound well-trimmed pork
  tenderloin, cut into ³/₄-inch
  medallions

1 tablespoon all-purpose flour

1 teaspoon ground cumin

1 teaspoon paprika

¹/₄ teaspoon powdered saffron *or*
  ¹/₂ teaspoon turmeric

¹/₄ teaspoon ground red pepper

¹/₄ teaspoon ground ginger

1 tablespoon olive oil

1 medium onion, chopped

3 cloves garlic, minced

2¹/₂ cups canned chicken broth,
  divided

¹/₃ cup golden or dark raisins

1 cup quick-cooking couscous

¹/₄ cup chopped fresh cilantro

¹/₄ cup sliced toasted almonds
  (optional)

1. Toss pork with flour, cumin, paprika, saffron, pepper and ginger in medium bowl; set aside.

2. Heat oil in large nonstick skillet over medium-high heat. Add onion; cook 5 minutes, stirring occasionally. Add pork and garlic; cook 4 to 5 minutes or until pork is no longer pink, stirring occasionally. Add ¾ cup chicken broth and raisins; bring to a boil over high heat. Reduce heat to medium; simmer, uncovered, 7 to 8 minutes or until pork is cooked through, stirring occasionally.

3. Meanwhile, bring remaining 1¾ cups chicken broth to a boil in medium saucepan. Stir in couscous. Cover; remove from heat. Let stand 5 minutes or until liquid is absorbed.

4. Spoon couscous onto 4 plates; top with pork mixture. Sprinkle with cilantro and almonds, if desired.

Makes 4 servings

*Food*Fact

Tagine is a meat and vegetable stew that gets its name from the conical earthenware pots historically used in North Africa as cooking vessels. The tight-fitting lid has a hole in the top that allows steam to escape at a consistent rate.

Moroccan Pork Tagine

2 tablespoons butter

3 medium onions, thinly sliced and separated into rings

1 package (1.0 ounce) LAWRY'S® Au Jus Gravy Mix

3 cups water

4 thin slices sourdough French bread

Unsalted butter, softened

4 slices Swiss or Gruyère cheese

French Onion Soup

In large skillet, heat 2 tablespoons butter. Add onions and cook over medium-high heat until golden. In small bowl, combine Au Jus Gravy Mix and water; add to onions. Bring to a boil over medium-high heat; reduce heat to low; cover and simmer 15 minutes, stirring occasionally. Broil bread on one side until lightly toasted. Turn bread slices over; spread with softened butter. Top with cheese; broil until cheese melts.

Makes 4 servings

Serving Suggestion: To serve, pour soup into tureen or individual bowls. Top each serving with toast.

Quick Tip

If using individual ovenproof bowls, pour soup into bowls; top with a slice of untoasted bread. Top with cheese. Place under broiler just until the cheese is melted.

French Onion Soup

6 tablespoons shredded sweetened coconut

1½ pound butternut squash

12 ounces boneless skinless chicken breasts

1 teaspoon olive oil

1 large onion, chopped

4 cloves garlic, minced

3 cans (about 14 ounces each) low-fat reduced-sodium chicken broth

2 jalapeño peppers,* stemmed, seeded and minced

2 teaspoons dried thyme leaves

½ package (10 ounces) spinach leaves, washed and torn

*Jalapeño peppers can sting and irritate the skin; wear rubber gloves when handling peppers and do not touch eyes. Wash hands after handling.

Caribbean Callaloo Soup

1. Preheat oven to 350°F. Place coconut in baking pan; bake 6 minutes, stirring every 2 minutes, until golden. Set aside. Peel squash; cut in half lengthwise and discard seeds. Cut into ½-inch cubes. Slice chicken crosswise into very thin strips.

2. Heat oil in large nonstick skillet over medium-low heat. Add onion and garlic; cook, covered, stirring often, 5 minutes or until onion is tender. Add squash, chicken broth, jalapeño peppers and thyme; bring to a boil over high heat. Reduce heat to low; simmer, covered, 15 to 20 minutes, until squash is very tender. Add chicken; cover and cook 2 minutes or until chicken is no longer pink in center. Remove skillet from heat; stir in spinach until wilted. Ladle into bowls and sprinkle with toasted coconut.   *Makes 6 servings*

Italian Bread Soup

1   can (28 ounces) whole tomatoes, undrained, cut up

2   cans (14½ ounces each) beef broth

1   package (1.5 ounces) LAWRY'S® Original-Style Spaghetti Sauce Spices & Seasonings

2   cups packaged cheese and garlic croutons, lightly crushed

1   tablespoon olive oil

2   teaspoons chopped fresh sage *or* ¾ teaspoon dried sage

¼   teaspoon pepper

     Whole fresh sage leaves (garnish)

     Additional croutons (garnish)

In large saucepan, combine tomatoes with juice, beef broth, Original-Style Spaghetti Sauce Spices & Seasonings and croutons. Bring to a boil over medium-high heat; reduce heat to low and simmer, uncovered, 15 minutes, stirring frequently. Add remaining ingredients and simmer 5 minutes longer.

Makes 4 to 6 servings

Serving Suggestion: Serve in shallow soup bowls. Garnish with whole sage leaves and croutons.

*Quick*Tip

Soup should be thick enough to "grab" a spoon. If it becomes too thick, stir in additional broth or water.

67

HEARTY *soups & stews*

Albóndigas Soup

1   pound ground beef

¼   cup long-grain rice

1   egg

1   tablespoon chopped fresh cilantro

1   teaspoon LAWRY'S® Seasoned Salt

¼   cup ice water

2   cans (14½ ounces each) chicken broth

1   can (14½ ounces) whole peeled tomatoes, undrained and cut up

1   stalk celery, diced

1   large carrot, diced

1   medium potato, diced

¼   cup chopped onion

¼   teaspoon LAWRY'S® Garlic Powder with Parsley

In medium bowl, combine ground beef, rice, egg, cilantro, Seasoned Salt and ice water; mix well and form into small meatballs. In large saucepan, combine broth, tomatoes with juice, celery, carrot, potato, onion and Garlic Powder with Parsley. Bring to a boil over medium-high heat; add meatballs. Reduce heat to low; cover and cook 30 to 40 minutes, stirring occasionally.   *Makes 6 to 8 servings*

Serving Suggestion: Serve with lemon wedges and warm tortillas.

*Quick*Tip

This soup gets its name from the word "albóndiga," the Spanish word for meatball. For a lower salt version, use homemade chicken broth or low-sodium chicken broth.

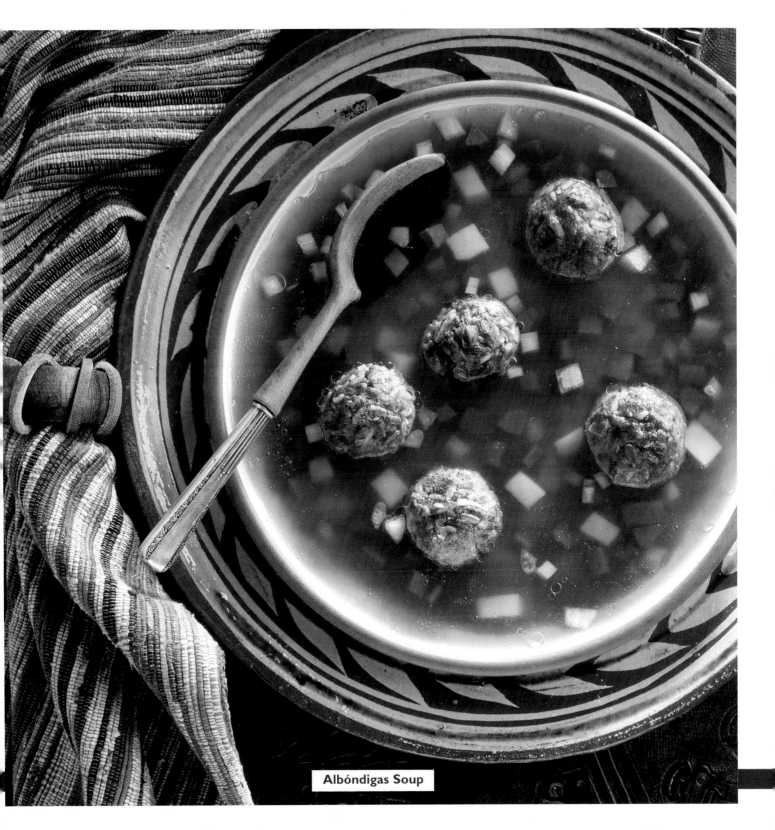

Albóndigas Soup

Italian Vegetable Stew

1 teaspoon olive or vegetable oil

2 medium zucchini, halved
lengthwise and thinly sliced

1 medium eggplant, chopped

1 large onion, thinly sliced

⅛ teaspoon ground black pepper

1 jar (26 to 28 ounces) RAGÚ®
Light Pasta Sauce

3 tablespoons grated Parmesan
cheese

1 box (10 ounces) couscous

1. In 12-inch nonstick skillet, heat oil over medium heat and cook zucchini, eggplant, onion and pepper, stirring occasionally, 15 minutes or until vegetables are golden.

2. Stir in Ragú Pasta Sauce and cheese. Bring to a boil over high heat. Reduce heat to low and simmer covered 10 minutes.

3. Meanwhile, prepare couscous according to package directions. Serve vegetable mixture over hot couscous.

Makes 4 servings

Prep Time: 10 minutes
Cook Time: 25 minutes

Italian Vegetable Stew

Cuban Chicken Bean Soup

8	chicken thighs, skinned, fat trimmed
8	cups water
2	cloves garlic, minced
2	teaspoons salt
2	bay leaves
1	cup chopped green bell pepper
1	cup chopped onion
2	cans (16 ounces each) black beans, drained and rinsed
2	tablespoons lime juice
1¼	teaspoons ground cumin
1	teaspoon sugar
½	teaspoon dried oregano leaves
½	teaspoon hot pepper sauce
1¼	cups cooked rice
¼	cup sliced green onions

In large saucepan or Dutch oven, place chicken; add water, garlic, salt and bay leaves. Cook over medium-high heat until mixture boils; cover, reduce heat to low and cook about 35 minutes or until chicken is fork-tender. Remove chicken; set aside. Chill broth until fat solidifies and can be skimmed from surface. Separate meat from bones; cut into bite-size pieces and set aside. To skimmed broth in same pan, add green pepper and onion; cook over medium heat 10 minutes or until vegetables are crisp-tender. Add chicken, black beans, lime juice, cumin, sugar and oregano. Cook over medium heat 10 minutes. Remove bay leaves. Stir in hot pepper sauce. Place 2 tablespoons cooked rice in individual bowls; ladle soup over rice. Sprinkle with green onions.

Makes 10 (1-cup) servings

Favorite recipe from **Delmarva Poultry Industry, Inc.**

Italian-Style Lamb Shanks

6 lamb shanks, about ³/₄ pound
   each

1 to 2 tablespoons salad oil

1 package (3 ounces) LAWRY'S®
   Original-Style Spaghetti Sauce
   Spices & Seasonings

2 cans (8 ounces each) tomato
   sauce

3 cups water

¹/₄ cup salad oil

2 medium onions, cut into
   ¹/₄-inch-thick slices

   Cooked wide egg noodles

Rub lamb shanks with 1 to 2 tablespoons oil; arrange in single layer in heavy roasting pan. Brown shanks in 450°F. oven, uncovered, 30 minutes, turning occasionally to brown evenly. Meanwhile, prepare Original-Style Spaghetti Sauce Spices & Seasonings according to package directions using tomato sauce, water and ¹/₄ cup salad oil. Once browned, remove shanks from oven and top with sliced onions. Pour spaghetti sauce over shanks. Cover; reduce heat to 375°F. and return to oven. Cook 1 hour or until tender, basting occasionally. Serve with egg noodles. *Makes 6 servings*

HEARTY soups & stews

1   cup dried lentils

2   tablespoons olive oil

1   onion, chopped

1   red bell pepper, chopped

1   teaspoon fennel seed

$\frac{1}{2}$ teaspoon ground cumin

$\frac{1}{4}$ teaspoon ground red pepper

4   cups water

$\frac{1}{2}$ teaspoon salt

1   tablespoon lemon juice

$\frac{1}{2}$ cup plain low-fat yogurt

2   tablespoons chopped fresh
    parsley

Middle Eastern Lentil Soup

1. Rinse lentils, discarding any debris or blemished lentils; drain. Heat oil in large saucepan over medium-high heat until hot. Add onion and bell pepper; cook and stir 5 minutes or until tender. Add fennel seed, cumin and ground red pepper; cook and stir 1 minute.

2. Add water and lentils. Bring to a boil. Reduce heat to low. Cover and simmer 20 minutes. Stir in salt. Simmer 5 to 10 minutes or until lentils are tender. Stir in lemon juice.

3. To serve, ladle soup into individual bowls and top with yogurt; sprinkle with parsley.   *Makes 4 servings*

*Quick*Tip

For a special touch, top each serving with yellow bell pepper strips.

Middle Eastern Lentil Soup

Sauerkraut Stew

2 pounds well-trimmed kosher flanken (beef short ribs)

1 package (2 pounds) HEBREW NATIONAL® Sauerkraut, undrained

2 cans (16 ounces each) diced tomatoes in juice, undrained

1 large potato, peeled, cut into $^1\!/_2$-inch pieces

$1^3\!/_4$ cups water, divided

$^1\!/_2$ teaspoon freshly ground black pepper

$^1\!/_2$ cup packed light brown sugar

2 tablespoons all-purpose flour

Combine flanken, sauerkraut, tomatoes with juice, potato, 1 1/2 cups water and pepper in Dutch oven. Cover; bring to a boil over high heat. Reduce heat to low; simmer 2 hours or until meat is tender.

Transfer meat to cutting board; cool slightly. Skim fat from surface of stew; discard fat. Stir brown sugar into stew. Combine flour and remaining 1/4 cup cold water in small glass measuring cup; stir into stew.

Discard bones and fat from meat; cut meat into 1/2-inch pieces. Stir into stew; simmer 5 minutes or until stew thickens.

Makes 6 to 8 servings

Wonton Soup

1/4 pound lean ground pork

2 ounces medium-size raw shrimp, peeled, deveined and minced

2 tablespoons minced green onions and tops

4 teaspoons KIKKOMAN® Soy Sauce, divided

1/2 teaspoon cornstarch

1/4 teaspoon grated fresh ginger root

24 wonton wrappers

4 cups water

3 cans (about 14 ounces each) chicken broth

1/4 cup dry sherry

1/2 pound bok choy cabbage

2 tablespoons chopped green onions and tops

1/2 teaspoon Oriental sesame oil

Combine pork, shrimp, minced green onions, 2 teaspoons soy sauce, cornstarch and ginger in medium bowl; mix well. Arrange several wonton wrappers on clean surface; cover remaining wrappers to prevent drying out. Place 1 teaspoonful pork mixture in center of each wrapper. Fold wrapper over filling to form a triangle. Gently fold center point down and moisten left corner with water. Twist and overlap opposite corner over moistened corner; press firmly to seal. Repeat with remaining wrappers. Bring water to boil in large saucepan. Add wontons. Boil gently 3 minutes; remove with slotted spoon. Discard water. Pour broth and sherry into same saucepan. Cut bok choy crosswise into 1/2-inch slices, separating stems from leaves. Add stems to broth mixture; bring to boil. Add cooked wontons; simmer 1 minute. Add bok choy leaves and chopped green onions; simmer 1 minute longer. Remove from heat; stir in remaining 2 teaspoons soy sauce and sesame oil. Serve immediately.

Makes 6 servings

Mexicali Chicken Stew

1   package (1.25 ounces) taco
    seasoning, divided

12 ounces boneless skinless chicken
    thighs

2   cans (14½ ounces each) stewed
    tomatoes with onions, celery
    and green peppers

1   package (9 ounces) frozen green
    beans

1   package (10 ounces) frozen corn

4   cups tortilla chips

1. Place half of taco seasoning in small bowl. Cut chicken thighs into 1-inch pieces; coat with taco seasoning.

2. Coat large nonstick skillet with cooking spray. Cook and stir chicken 5 minutes over medium heat. Add tomatoes, beans, corn and remaining taco seasoning; bring to a boil. Reduce heat to medium-low; simmer 10 minutes. Top with tortilla chips before serving.   *Makes 4 servings*

Serving Suggestion: Serve nachos with stew. Spread tortilla chips on plate; dot with salsa and sprinkle with cheese. Heat just until cheese is melted.

Prep and Cook Time: 20 minutes

*Quick*Tip

To lighten up this dish, simply substitute boneless skinless chicken breasts for the thighs. Each cup of cooked light meat has 44 less calories and 8 less grams of fat than a cup of dark meat.

Mexicali Chicken Stew

Short Rib Soup (Kalbitang)

2 pounds beef short ribs or flanken-style ribs

2 quarts water

2 tablespoons dried cloud ear or other Oriental mushrooms

1/2 cup thinly sliced green onions

3 tablespoons soy sauce

2 tablespoons Sesame Salt*

2 cloves garlic, peeled and cut into slivers to measure 1 tablespoon

1/2 teaspoon sesame oil

1/4 teaspoon red pepper flakes

1 egg, lightly beaten

1 bunch chives

*To make Sesame Salt, crush 1/2 cup toasted sesame seeds and 1/4 teaspoon salt with mortar and pestle or process in clean coffee or spice grinder.

1. Score both sides of ribs in diamond pattern with tip of sharp knife. Bring ribs and water to boil in stockpot or 5-quart Dutch oven over high heat. Reduce heat to medium; frequently skim foam that rises to surface until broth is clear. Reduce heat to medium-low; cook, uncovered, about 1½ hours or until meat is tender. Remove ribs from broth; let cool slightly.

2. Place mushrooms in bowl; cover with hot water. Let stand 30 minutes or until caps are soft. Drain mushrooms; squeeze out excess water. Remove and discard stems. Thinly slice caps.

3. To degrease broth, let stand 5 minutes so fat rises. Quickly pull paper towel across surface of broth, allowing towel to absorb fat. Repeat with clean paper towels as many times as necessary to remove all fat. (Or refrigerate broth for several hours or overnight and remove fat that rises to surface.)

4. Cut meat from ribs with utility knife; discard bones and gristle. Cut meat into bite-size pieces. Combine beef, mushrooms, green onions, soy sauce, Sesame Salt, garlic, sesame oil and red pepper flakes in medium bowl. Add beef mixture to degreased beef broth; cook 15 minutes over medium-low heat.

5. Meanwhile, spray 7-inch omelet pan or small skillet with nonstick cooking spray. Pour egg into pan; cook over medium-high heat until set on both sides. Let cool. Cut circles from omelet with round cookie cutter. Cut crescent shapes from circles with edge of round cookie cutter. serve soup, garnished with omelet crescents and chives.

Makes 4 servings

Short Rib Soup (Kalbitang)

2 cups water

1 package KNORR® Recipe Classics™ Vegetable or Spring Vegetable Soup, Dip and Recipe Mix

1 bottle or can (8 to 10 ounces) clam juice

2 teaspoons tomato paste

1/2 teaspoon paprika

1/4 teaspoon saffron threads (optional)

12 mussels or clams, well scrubbed

1 1/2 pounds mixed seafood (cubed cod, snapper, scallops or shrimp)

Bouillabaisse

• In 3-quart saucepan, bring water, recipe mix, clam juice, tomato paste, paprika and saffron to a boil over medium-high heat, stirring occasionally.

• Add mussels and seafood. Bring to a boil over high heat.

• Reduce heat to low and simmer 5 minutes or until shells open and seafood is cooked through and flakes easily when tested with a fork. Discard any unopened shells.

Makes 6 servings

Prep Time: 15 minutes
Cook Time: 10 minutes

*Quick*Tip

To clean mussels, scrub with a stiff brush under cold running water. To debeard mussels, pull the threads from the shells with your fingers. Mussels die soon after debearding. Use them immediately.

Bouillabaisse

Olive oil-flavored nonstick cooking spray

1/2 pound boneless skinless chicken breasts, cut into 1/2-inch pieces

1 large onion, diced

3 cans (14 1/2 ounces each) chicken broth

1 can (15 ounces) whole tomatoes, undrained

1 can (14 ounces) Great Northern beans, rinsed and drained

2 medium carrots, sliced

1 large potato, diced

1/4 teaspoon salt

1/4 teaspoon black pepper

1 cup frozen Italian green beans

1/4 cup prepared pesto

Grated Parmesan cheese (optional)

Chicken Soup au Pistou

Spray large saucepan with cooking spray; heat over medium-high heat until hot. Add chicken; cook and stir about 5 minutes or until chicken is browned. Add onion; cook and stir 2 minutes.

Add chicken broth, tomatoes with juice, Great Northern beans, carrots, potato, salt and pepper. Bring to a boil, stirring to break up tomatoes. Reduce heat to low. Cover and simmer 15 minutes, stirring occasionally. Add green beans; cook about 5 minutes more or until vegetables are tender.

Ladle soup into bowls. Top each serving with 1 1/2 teaspoons pesto and sprinkle with Parmesan cheese, if desired.

Makes about 12 cups or 8 servings

Chicken Soup au Pistou

1 pound BOB EVANS® Original Recipe or Zesty Hot Roll Sausage

1½ tablespoons olive oil

½ small Spanish onion, diced

1 jalapeño pepper, seeded and diced

1½ cups beef broth

1 cup peeled, seeded and diced fresh or canned tomatoes

1 cup vegetable juice

½ tablespoon ground cumin

½ tablespoon chili powder

¼ teaspoon salt

⅓ cup shredded Cheddar cheese

12 tortilla chips, broken into pieces

Taco Soup

Crumble and cook sausage in olive oil in Dutch oven until no longer pink but not yet browned. Add onion and pepper; cook until onion is tender. Add remaining ingredients except cheese and chips; bring to a boil over high heat. Reduce heat to low and simmer, uncovered, 15 minutes. Ladle soup into bowls; garnish with cheese and chips. Refrigerate leftovers.

Makes 6 servings

*Quick*Tip

To remove a sausage casing, use a paring knife to slit the casing at one end. Be careful not to cut through the sausage. Grasp the cut edge and gently pull the casing away from the sausage.

Taco Soup

Hanoi Beef and Rice Soup

1½ pounds ground beef chuck

2 tablespoons cold water

2 tablespoons soy sauce

2 teaspoons sugar

2 teaspoons cornstarch

2 teaspoons lime juice

½ teaspoon black pepper

2 cloves garlic, minced

2 teaspoons fennel seeds

1 teaspoon anise seeds

1 cinnamon stick (3 inches long)

2 bay leaves

6 whole cloves

1 tablespoon vegetable oil

1 cup uncooked long-grain white rice

1 medium yellow onion, sliced and separated into rings

1 tablespoon minced fresh ginger

4 cans (about 14 ounces each) beef broth

2 cups water

½ pound fresh snow peas, trimmed

1 fresh red Thai chili or red jalapeño pepper, cut into slivers, for garnish

1. Combine beef, 2 tablespoons water, soy sauce, sugar, cornstarch, lime juice, black pepper and garlic in large bowl; mix well. Place meat mixture on cutting board; pat evenly into 1-inch-thick square. Cut meat into 36 squares; shape each square into a ball.

2. Bring 4 inches water to a boil in wok over high heat. Add meatballs and return water to a boil. Cook meatballs 3 to 4 minutes or until firm, stirring occasionally. Transfer meatballs to bowl with slotted spoon. Discard water.

3. Place fennel seeds, anise seeds, cinnamon, bay leaves and cloves on 12-inch double-thick square of dampened cheesecloth. Tie with string into spice bag; set aside.

4. Heat wok over medium heat 1 minute or until hot. Drizzle oil into wok and heat 30 seconds. Add rice; cook and stir 3 to 4 minutes or until lightly browned. Add onion and ginger. Stir-fry 1 minute. Add beef broth, 2 cups water and spice bag. Cover and bring to a boil. Reduce heat to low; simmer 25 minutes.

5. Remove spice bag and discard. Add meatballs and snow peas to soup. Cook and stir until heated through. Ladle soup into tureen or individual serving bowls. Garnish, if desired.

Makes 6 main-dish servings

Hanoi Beef and Rice Soup

$^1/_4$ cup all-purpose flour

1 tablespoon Hungarian sweet paprika

$1^1/_2$ teaspoons salt

$^1/_2$ teaspoon Hungarian hot paprika

$^1/_2$ teaspoon black pepper

2 pounds beef stew meat ($1^1/_4$-inch pieces)

4 tablespoons vegetable oil, divided

1 large onion, chopped

4 cloves garlic, minced

2 cans (about 14 ounces each) beef broth

1 can ($14^1/_2$ ounces) stewed tomatoes, undrained

1 cup water

1 tablespoon dried marjoram leaves, crushed

1 large green bell pepper, chopped

3 cups uncooked thin egg noodle twists

  Sour cream

Hungarian Beef Goulash

1. Combine flour, sweet paprika, salt, hot paprika and black pepper in resealable plastic food storage bag. Add $^1/_2$ of beef. Seal bag; shake to coat well. Repeat with remaining beef.

2. Heat $4^1/_2$ teaspoons oil in Dutch oven over medium heat until hot. Add $^1/_2$ of beef; brown on all sides. Transfer to large bowl. Repeat with $4^1/_2$ teaspoons oil and remaining beef; transfer to same bowl.

3. Heat remaining 1 tablespoon oil in same Dutch oven; add onion and garlic. Cook 8 minutes or until tender, stirring often.

4. Return beef and any juices to Dutch oven. Add broth, tomatoes with juice, water and marjoram. Bring to a boil over medium-high heat. Reduce heat to medium-low; cover and simmer $1^1/_2$ hours or until meat is tender, stirring once.

5. When meat is tender, stir in bell pepper and noodles; cover. Simmer about 8 minutes or until noodles are tender, stirring once. To serve, ladle into 8 soup bowls. Dollop with sour cream.

Makes 8 servings

Hungarian Beef Goulash

4 tablespoons olive or vegetable oil, divided

2 cups diced carrots

3 medium zucchini and/or yellow squash, diced

1 jar (26 to 28 ounces) RAGÚ® Light Pasta Sauce

2 cans (13¾ ounces each) chicken or vegetable broth

1 can (19 ounces) cannellini or white kidney beans, rinsed and drained

1 cup packed fresh basil leaves

1 large clove garlic, finely chopped

¼ teaspoon salt

Summer Minestrone with Pesto

In 5-quart saucepan, heat 1 tablespoon oil over medium-high heat and cook carrots and zucchini, stirring occasionally, 8 minutes. Stir in Ragú® Light Pasta Sauce and chicken broth. Bring to a boil over high heat. Reduce heat to low and simmer covered, stirring occasionally, 20 minutes or until vegetables are tender. Stir in beans; heat through.

Meanwhile, for pesto, in blender or food processor, blend basil, garlic, salt and remaining 3 tablespoons oil until basil is finely chopped. To serve, ladle soup into bowls and garnish each with spoonful of pesto. *Makes 8 (1-cup) servings*

*Quick*Tip

During the winter months, fresh basil can be found in small plastic packages in the produce section of the supermarket. Place the basil, stems down, in a glass of water with a plastic bag over the leaves; refrigerate for up to a week, changing the water occasionally.

Summer Minestrone with Pesto

2 cans (about 14 ounces each) fat-free reduced-sodium chicken broth

4 ounces boneless pork loin, sliced into thin strips

3/4 cup thinly sliced mushrooms

1/2 cup firm tofu, cut into 1/4-inch cubes (optional)

3 tablespoons white vinegar

3 tablespoons sherry

1 tablespoon reduced-sodium soy sauce

1/2 teaspoon ground red pepper

2 ounces uncooked low-fat ramen noodles

1 egg, beaten

1/4 cup finely chopped green onions, green tops only

Asian Ramen Noodle Soup

1. Bring chicken broth to a boil in large saucepan over high heat; add pork, mushrooms and tofu, if desired. Reduce heat to medium-low; simmer, covered, 5 minutes. Stir in vinegar, sherry, soy sauce and pepper.

2. Return broth mixture to a boil over high heat; stir in ramen noodles. Cook, stirring occasionally, 5 to 7 minutes or until noodles are tender. Slowly stir in beaten egg and green onions; remove from heat. Ladle soup into individual bowls.

Makes 4 (3/4-cup) servings

FoodFact

Tofu, also known as soybean curd, is made by coagulating soy milk, draining it and pressing the curds in a method similar to cheesemaking. Used extensively in Asian cooking, tofu is white or cream-colored with a creamy smooth texture. It has a bland, slightly nutty taste, but readily takes on the flavor of foods it is cooked with. It is available in three forms: soft, firm and extra firm. Soft tofu can be whipped or blended for use in dips, fillings and scrambled eggs. Firm and extra-firm tofu can be cubed and used in stir-fries.

Asian Ramen Noodle Soup

3 cups water

$^{1}/_{2}$ pound boneless skinless chicken breast halves, cut into $^{1}/_{2}$-inch pieces

1 cup chopped fresh tomatoes *or* 1 can (8 ounces) whole peeled tomatoes, undrained and chopped

1 pouch LIPTON® Soup Secrets Noodle Soup Mix with Real Chicken Broth

$^{1}/_{2}$ teaspoon LAWRY'S® Garlic Powder with Parsley (optional)

$^{1}/_{2}$ cup shredded mozzarella cheese (about 2 ounces)

Grated Parmesan cheese (optional)

Noodle Soup Parmigiano

In medium saucepan, combine all ingredients except cheeses; bring to a boil. Reduce heat and simmer uncovered, stirring occasionally, 5 minutes or until chicken is done. To serve, spoon into bowls; sprinkle with cheeses.

Makes about 5 (1-cup) servings

*Food*Fact

Cheese, said the ancient Greeks, was a gift from benevolent gods. Then, as now, cheese was a means of preserving milk, making it a useful, versatile food. Cheesemaking has evolved into an art practiced around the world. There are hundreds of types available today, each with its own distinctive flavor and texture.

Southern Italian Clam Chowder

2 slices bacon, diced

1 cup chopped onion

$1/2$ cup chopped peeled carrots

$1/2$ cup chopped celery

2 cans (14.5 ounces each) CONTADINA® Recipe Ready Diced Tomatoes, undrained

1 can (8 ounces) CONTADINA® Tomato Sauce

1 bottle (8 ounces) clam juice

$1/2$ teaspoon chopped fresh rosemary or $1/4$ teaspoon dried rosemary leaves, crushed

$1/8$ teaspoon ground black pepper

2 cans ($6^1/2$ ounces each) chopped clams, undrained

1. Sauté bacon in large saucepan until crisp. Add onion, carrots and celery; sauté for 2 to 3 minutes or until vegetables are tender.

2. Stir in tomatoes and juice, tomato sauce, clam juice, rosemary and pepper. Bring to a boil.

3. Reduce heat to low; simmer, uncovered, 15 minutes. Stir in clams and juice. Simmer 5 minutes or until heated through.

Makes 8 cups

Prep Time: 8 minutes
Cook Time: 23 minutes

Any collection of soups would be incomplete without an offering of cream-based selections. Truly the **cream of the crop,** *abundantly rich and* **deliciously decadent,** *these cream soups are sure to satisfy the most hearty appetites.*

Potato-Crab Chowder

1 cup frozen hash brown potatoes

1 package (10 ounces) frozen corn

$3/4$ cup finely chopped carrots

1 teaspoon dried thyme leaves

$3/4$ teaspoon garlic-pepper seasoning

3 cups fat-free reduced-sodium chicken broth

$1/2$ cup water

1 cup evaporated milk

3 tablespoons cornstarch

$1/2$ cup sliced green onion

1 can (6 ounces) crabmeat, drained

1. Place potatoes, corn and carrots in slow cooker. Sprinkle with thyme and garlic-pepper seasoning.

2. Add broth and water. Cover and cook on LOW for $3\frac{1}{2}$ to $4\frac{1}{2}$ hours.

3. Stir together evaporated milk and cornstarch in medium bowl. Stir into slow cooker. Turn temperature to HIGH. Cover and cook 1 hour. Stir in green onions and crabmeat. Garnish as desired.

Makes 5 servings

Potato-Crab Chowder

Nonstick cooking spray

1   teaspoon extra-virgin olive oil

2   cups chopped yellow onions

1   cup thinly sliced carrots

2   cans (about 14 ounces each) fat-free reduced-sodium chicken broth

1   can (10³/₄ ounces) 98% fat-free cream of mushroom soup

12 ounces sliced mushrooms

¹/₂ cup quick-cooking barley

1   teaspoon reduced-sodium Worcestershire sauce

¹/₂ teaspoon dried thyme leaves

¹/₄ cup finely chopped green onions

¹/₄ teaspoon salt

¹/₄ teaspoon black pepper

Hearty Mushroom Barley Soup

Heat Dutch oven or large saucepan over medium-high heat until hot. Coat with cooking spray. Add oil and tilt pan to coat bottom of pan. Add yellow onions; cook 8 minutes or until just beginning to turn golden. Add carrots and cook 2 minutes.

Add broth, cream of mushroom soup, mushrooms, barley, Worcestershire sauce and thyme; bring to a boil over high heat. Reduce heat to medium-low; cover and simmer 15 minutes, stirring occasionally. Stir in green onions, salt and pepper. Garnish as desired.   *Makes 4 (1¹/₂-cup) servings*

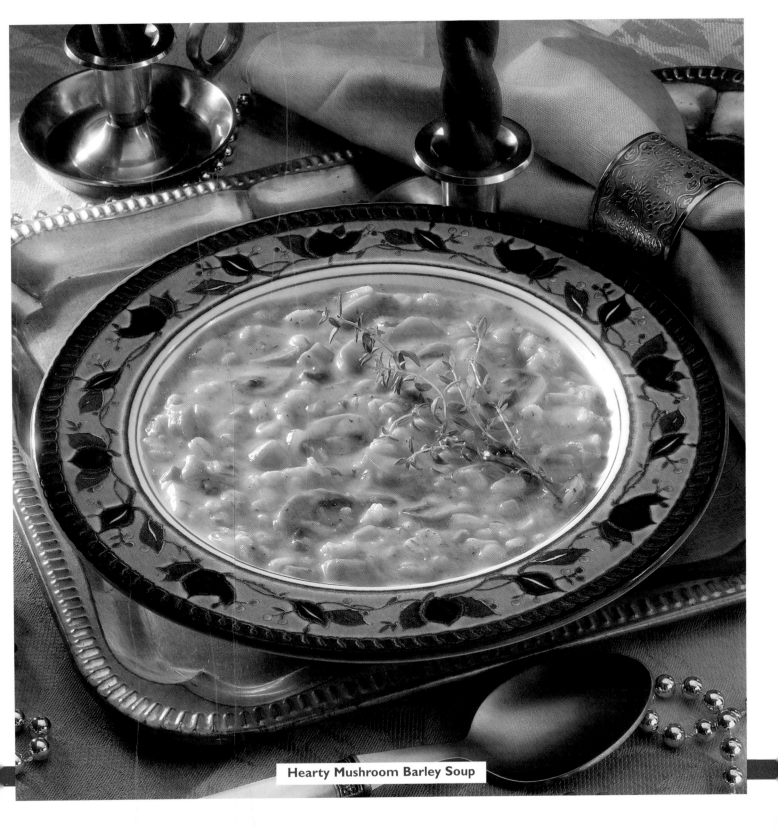

Hearty Mushroom Barley Soup

½ cup uncooked wild rice

5 cups canned chicken broth, divided

¼ cup butter

1 large carrot, sliced

1 medium onion, chopped

2 ribs celery, chopped

¼ pound fresh mushrooms, sliced

2 tablespoons all-purpose flour

¼ teaspoon salt

¼ teaspoon white pepper

1½ cups chopped cooked chicken

¼ cup dry sherry

Cream of Chicken and Wild Rice Soup

1. Rinse rice thoroughly in fine strainer under cold running water; drain.

2. Combine 2½ cups chicken broth and rice in 2-quart saucepan. Bring to a boil over medium-high heat. Reduce heat to low; simmer, covered, 1 hour or until rice is tender. Drain; set aside.

3. Melt butter in 3-quart saucepan over medium heat. Add carrot; cook and stir 3 minutes. Add onion, celery and mushrooms; cook and stir 3 to 4 minutes or until vegetables are tender. Remove from heat. Whisk in flour, salt and pepper until smooth.

4. Gradually stir in remaining 2½ cups chicken broth. Bring to a boil over medium heat; cook and stir 1 minute or until thickened. Stir in chicken and sherry. Reduce heat to low; simmer, uncovered, 3 minutes or until heated through.

5. Spoon ¼ cup cooked rice into each serving bowl. Ladle soup over rice. *Makes 4 to 6 servings*

Cream of Chicken and Wild Rice Soup

Cream of Portobello Soup
...without the Cream

1 pound potatoes, peeled, cut in
   ½-inch cubes (about 3 cups)

3 tablespoons butter

2 large carrots chopped (about
   1 cup)

1 large onion chopped (about
   1 cup)

1 teaspoon minced garlic

1 pound portobello mushrooms,
   coarsely chopped* (about
   6 cups)

¼ cup dry sherry

1½ cups milk

1 cup chicken broth

½ teaspoon salt

½ teaspoon dried thyme leaves

Pinch ground black pepper

If using portobellos with stems, trim and coarsely chop.

In large saucepan, add potatoes and 3 cups water. Cook, covered, over medium-high heat until tender, about 10 minutes; drain and set aside. In large skillet over medium-high heat, melt butter. Add carrots, onion and garlic; cook, stirring frequently, until barely tender, about 5 minutes. Add mushrooms; cook and stir until mushrooms are tender, about 5 minutes. Stir in sherry; cook 1 minute. Remove 1½ cups mushroom mixture; set aside. In food processor, place potatoes and remaining mushroom mixture from skillet. Process until smooth. Pour into saucepan. Add milk, broth, salt, thyme, pepper and reserved 1½ cups mushroom mixture. Simmer over medium heat until heated through, about 10 minutes.   *Makes 6½ cups*

Favorite recipe from **Mushroom Council**

FoodFact

Portobello mushrooms are actually the mature form of cremini mushrooms. They are firm and dense in texture and beeflike in flavor, making them an excellent vegetarian substitute for meat ingredients in many dishes.

Pasta and Vegetable Chowder

2½ cups rainbow-colored rotini

6 slices bacon, cut into 1-inch pieces

1 cup chopped onions

½ cup 1-inch celery pieces

3 tablespoons all-purpose flour

6 cups chicken broth, divided

3 cups zucchini (2 cups shredded, 1 diced)

¾ cup sliced carrots

1 cup skim milk

¼ cup chopped celery leaves

½ teaspoon pepper

Cook pasta according to package directions; drain.

Cook bacon in large saucepan until crisp. Remove bacon from saucepan; drain all but 1 tablespoon bacon drippings from saucepan. Add onions and celery to saucepan; cook and stir until crisp-tender.

Add flour to 1 cup chicken broth in small bowl; mix until smooth. Add to ingredients in saucepan. Gradually stir in remaining broth; bring to a boil. Add shredded zucchini and carrots; return to a boil. Reduce heat to low; simmer 10 minutes. Add diced zucchini; simmer until vegetables are tender, about 12 minutes. Add cooked pasta, milk, celery leaves and pepper; bring to a boil and serve.

Makes 6 servings

Favorite recipe from **North Dakota Wheat Commission**

105

HEARTY *soups & stews*

OZOLE BISQUE CHOWDER CHILI BOUILLABAISSE GUMBO PISTOU CIOPPINO

HEARTY *soups & stews*

1 tablespoon margarine

1 cup chopped onion

2 tablespoons all-purpose flour

2½ cups fat-free reduced-sodium
   chicken broth

1 can (16 ounces) cream-style corn

1 cup frozen whole kernel corn

½ cup finely diced red bell pepper

½ teaspoon hot pepper sauce

¾ cup (3 ounces) shredded sharp
   Cheddar cheese

Black pepper (optional)

Double Corn & Cheddar Chowder

1. Melt margarine in large saucepan over medium heat. Add onion; cook and stir 5 minutes. Sprinkle onion with flour; cook and stir 1 minute.

2. Add chicken broth; bring to a boil, stirring frequently. Add cream-style corn, kernel corn, bell pepper and pepper sauce; bring to a simmer. Cover; simmer 15 minutes.

3. Remove from heat; gradually stir in cheese until melted. Ladle into soup bowls; sprinkle with black pepper, if desired. Garnish as desired. *Makes 6 servings*

Double Corn & Cheddar Chowder

Pumpkin Almond Bisque

1   medium-size pumpkin

3   cups chicken broth, divided

2   tablespoons butter or margarine

3   tablespoons chopped celery

3   tablespoons chopped onion

2   tablespoons almond paste

1   tablespoon tomato paste

1½   cups half-and-half

3   tablespoons almond-flavored
     liqueur

1   teaspoon ground nutmeg

1   teaspoon black pepper
     Salt to taste
     Toasted Pumpkin Seeds
     (recipe follows)

Cut slice from top of pumpkin. Scoop out seeds and fibers; reserve. Cut pumpkin into eight pieces and remove flesh from skin. Simmer pumpkin flesh in small amount of chicken broth until tender. Place cooked pumpkin in food processor or blender container; process until smooth. (There should be 2 cups pumpkin purée.) Leave purée in food processor.

Melt butter in heavy stockpot. Add celery and onion; cook over low heat 5 minutes. Add celery mixture, almond paste and tomato paste to pumpkin purée; process until smooth. Return contents of food processor to stockpot; add remaining broth and simmer over low heat, 30 minutes. Stir in half-and-half and cook until heated through. Stir in liqueur, nutmeg, pepper and salt. Serve garnished with Toasted Pumpkin Seeds.   *Makes about 8 servings*

Toasted Pumpkin Seeds: Preheat oven to 275°F. Carefully separate reserved seeds from fibers. Wash, drain and dry on paper towels. In small bowl, coat seeds with small amount of vegetable oil. Add 2 tablespoons Worcestershire sauce and ½ teaspoon ground red pepper; toss to mix thoroughly. Spread seasoned seeds in single layer on baking sheet. Bake, stirring occasionally, until golden brown.

Carrot Cream Soup

¼ cup butter or margarine

¼ cup chopped onion

½ teaspoon LAWRY'S® Garlic Powder with Parsley

¼ teaspoon LAWRY'S® Seasoned Salt

2 cups chopped carrots

½ cup all-purpose flour

4½ cups chicken broth

¼ cup whipping cream

Chopped fresh parsley for garnish

In large saucepan, heat butter. Add onion and cook over medium-high heat until tender. Add Garlic Powder with Parsley, Seasoned Salt and carrots; cook additional 5 minutes. Stir in flour; mix well. Stirring constantly, add chicken broth; mix well. Bring to a boil over medium-high heat; reduce heat to low and cook, covered, 30 minutes, stirring occasionally. In blender or food processor, purée carrot mixture; return to pan. Stir in cream; heat thoroughly. *Makes 4 servings*

Serving Suggestion: Serve warm soup topped with a sprinkling of parsley. Warm French bread or crackers are welcome accompaniments.

QuickTip

109

This soup may be prepared in advance. Refrigerate soup until chilled. To serve, purée the soup, add cream and cook over medium heat until heated through.

HEARTY soups & stews

Cheesy Potato Chowder

1½ cups water

3 medium red potatoes, peeled and cubed

1 rib celery, sliced

1 medium carrot, chopped

¼ cup butter or margarine

3 green onions, sliced

¼ cup all-purpose flour

1 teaspoon salt

⅛ teaspoon black pepper

4 cups milk

2 cups (8 ounces) shredded American cheese

1 cup (4 ounces) shredded Swiss cheese

½ teaspoon caraway seeds

Fresh chervil for garnish

Oyster crackers (optional)

1. Combine water, potatoes, celery and carrot in medium saucepan. Bring to a boil over high heat. Reduce heat to medium; simmer, uncovered, 10 minutes or until vegetables are tender.

2. Meanwhile, melt butter in large saucepan over medium heat. Cook and stir onions in butter 2 minutes or until tender but not brown. Stir in flour, salt and pepper. Cook and stir about 1 minute.

3. Stir milk and potato mixture into flour mixture; cook and stir over medium heat until bubbly. Cook and stir 1 minute more. Stir in cheeses and caraway seeds. Reduce heat to low; simmer, uncovered, until cheeses are melted and mixture is hot, stirring constantly. Garnish with chervil. Serve with oyster crackers, if desired. *Makes 6 servings*

Cheesy Potato Chowder

Creamy Garlic and Chestnut Soup

1 leek

1 tablespoon FILIPPO BERIO® Olive Oil

1 small onion, sliced

4 cloves garlic, peeled

2½ cups chicken broth

2 (8-ounce) cans peeled chestnuts, drained

½ cup half-and-half

Pinch grated nutmeg

Salt and freshly ground black pepper

Chopped fresh chives (optional)

Cut off root end and top of leek. Split leek; wash thoroughly and drain. Thinly slice white part of leek. In large saucepan, heat olive oil over medium heat until hot. Add leek, onion and garlic; cook and stir 5 minutes. Add chicken broth and chestnuts. Cover; reduce heat to low and simmer 15 minutes or until vegetables are tender. Cool slightly.

Process soup in small batches in blender or food processor until smooth. Return soup to saucepan; stir in half-and-half and nutmeg. Heat through. Season to taste with salt and pepper. Garnish with chives, if desired. Serve hot.

Makes 4 servings

Tex-Mex Cheddar Cheese Soup

2 cans (10¾ ounces each) condensed Cheddar cheese or cream of chicken soup

2 cups milk

1 cup half-and-half

2 cups shredded Cheddar cheese

1 can (4 ounces) green chilies, finely chopped

1 teaspoon ground cumin

2 cups *French's® Taste Toppers™* French Fried Onions

1. Combine soup, milk and half-and-half in large saucepan. Heat over medium-high heat until hot. Stir in cheese, chilies and cumin. Cook until cheese melts, stirring constantly.

2. Place **Taste Toppers** on microwave-safe dish. Microwave on HIGH 1 minute or until golden.

3. Spoon soup into bowls. Garnish with sour cream and fresh cilantro, if desired. Top with **Taste Toppers**.

Makes 6 servings

Prep Time: 5 minutes
Cook Time: 10 minutes

113

HEARTY soups & stews

Nita Lou's Cream of Broccoli Soup

1/3 cup plus 1 tablespoon WESSON® Vegetable Oil

3 cups coarsely chopped broccoli florets and stems

1 cup diced carrots

1 1/2 cups fresh chopped leeks

3 tablespoons all-purpose flour

1 1/2 teaspoons minced fresh garlic

2 (12-ounce) cans evaporated milk

1 1/2 cups homemade chicken stock or canned chicken broth

1/2 teaspoon garlic salt

1/4 teaspoon ground nutmeg

1/8 teaspoon pepper

3 tablespoons chopped fresh parsley

Salt to taste

In a large saucepan, heat *3 tablespoons* Wesson Oil. Add broccoli and carrots; sauté until tender. Remove vegetables; set aside. Add *remaining* oil, leeks, flour and garlic; sauté until leeks are limp and flour is lightly browned, about 2 minutes, stirring constantly. Whisk in evaporated milk and stock. Continue to cook, whisking constantly until flour has dissolved and mixture is smooth. *Do not bring mixture to a boil.* Reduce heat to low. Add cooked vegetables along with any juices, garlic salt, nutmeg and pepper. Simmer 5 minutes longer, being careful not to bring soup to a boil. Remove pan from heat; stir in parsley. Let soup stand 5 minutes before serving. Salt to taste. *Makes 6 servings*

Nita Lou's Cream of Broccoli Soup

Sweet Potato Bisque

1 pound sweet potatoes, peeled
2 teaspoons margarine
½ cup minced onion
1 teaspoon curry powder
½ teaspoon ground coriander
¼ teaspoon salt
⅔ cup unsweetened apple juice
1 cup low-fat buttermilk
¼ cup water
Plain low-fat yogurt for garnish (optional)

Bring 2 quarts water and potatoes to a boil in large saucepan over high heat. Cook, uncovered, 40 minutes or until potatoes are fork-tender. Drain; run under cold water until cool enough to handle.

Meanwhile, melt margarine in small saucepan over medium heat. Add onion; cook and stir 2 minutes. Stir in curry, coriander and salt; cook and stir about 45 seconds. Remove saucepan from heat; stir in apple juice. Set aside until potatoes have cooled.

Cut potatoes into pieces. Combine potatoes, buttermilk and onion mixture in food processor or blender; process until smooth. Pour soup back into large saucepan; stir in ¼ cup water to thin to desired consistency. (If soup is too thick, add 1 to 2 more tablespoons water.) Cook and stir over medium heat until heated through. Do not boil. Garnish each serving with dollop of yogurt, if desired. *Makes 4 servings*

Cheddar Vegetable Soup

1/4 cup vegetable oil

1 onion, chopped

1 large red bell pepper, chopped

1 teaspoon LAWRY'S® Garlic Powder with Parsley

2 white potatoes, peeled and cubed

2 zucchini, halved and sliced into 1/2-inch slices

1 package (16 ounces) frozen corn, thawed

1/3 cup all-purpose flour

4 cups chicken broth

2 cups milk

4 cups (16 ounces) grated shredded cheddar cheese

In Dutch oven, heat oil. Add onion, red pepper and Garlic Powder with Parsley and cook over medium-high heat until tender. Add potatoes, zucchini, and corn. Cook 3 minutes. Add flour; mix well. Slowly add broth; bring to a boil over medium-high heat, reduce heat to low, cover and simmer 10 minutes. Add milk and stir in cheese in batches. Heat until cheese is melted.   *Makes 6 servings*

Serving Suggestion: Serve with crusty bread sticks.

117

*Food*Fact

Natural cheeses are categorized by the amount of moisture they contain. Categories include hard cheese, such as Parmesan, with 30 percent moisture; firm, such as Cheddar, with 30 to 40 percent moisture; semisoft, such as Monterey Jack, with 40 to 50 percent moisture; soft and ripened, such as Brie, with 50 to 75 percent moisture; and soft and unripened, such as cream cheese, with 80 percent moisture.

HEARTY *soups & stews*

Farmhouse Ham and Vegetable Chowder

2   cans (10½ ounces each) cream
      of celery soup

2   cups diced cooked ham

1   package (10 ounces) frozen corn

1   large baking potato, cut in
      ½-inch pieces

1   medium red bell pepper, diced

½   teaspoon dried thyme leaves

2   cups small broccoli florets

½   cup milk

1. Combine all ingredients, except broccoli and milk in slow cooker; stir to blend. Cover and cook on LOW 6 to 8 hours or on HIGH 3 to 4 hours.

2. If cooking on LOW, turn to HIGH and stir in broccoli and milk. Cover and cook 15 minutes or until broccoli is crisp-tender.   *Makes 6 servings*

Farmhouse Ham and Vegetable Chowder

½ teaspoon olive oil

½ cup finely chopped onion

1 cup water

1½ teaspoons chicken bouillon granules

3 cups small broccoli florets or thawed frozen chopped broccoli

½ cup evaporated skimmed milk

⅛ teaspoon ground red pepper

2 ounces cubed light pasteurized process cheese product

¼ cup nonfat sour cream

⅛ teaspoon salt

Cheesy Broccoli Soup

1. Heat oil in medium saucepan over medium-high heat until hot. Add onion; cook and stir 4 minutes or until translucent.

2. Add water and bouillon granules; bring to a boil over high heat. Add broccoli; return to a boil. Reduce heat; simmer, covered, 5 minutes or until broccoli is tender.

3. Whisk in milk and red pepper. Remove from heat; stir in cheese until melted. Stir in sour cream and salt.

Makes 2 (1½-cup) servings

*Food*Fact

Though grown in Italy for centuries, broccoli didn't become popular in the United States until the 1920's when it began appearing in the home gardens of Italian immigrants. A member of the cabbage family, broccoli heads are made up of hundreds of buds, which if left to bloom, would open into yellow flowers. The majority of broccoli in the United States is grown in the Salinas Valley of California.

Corn & Red Pepper Soup

2 tablespoons butter or margarine

2 cups seeded and coarsely chopped red bell peppers

1 medium onion, thinly sliced

1 can (about 14 ounces) chicken broth

1 package (10 ounces) frozen whole kernel corn*

1/2 teaspoon ground cumin

1/2 cup sour cream

Salt

White pepper

Sunflower seeds for garnish

*Cut raw kernels from 4 large ears of yellow or white corn to substitute for frozen corn.

Melt butter in 3-quart saucepan over medium heat. Add bell peppers and onion; cook until tender. Add chicken broth, corn and cumin.

Bring to a boil over high heat. Reduce heat to low. Cover and simmer 20 minutes or until corn is tender.

Pour into food processor or blender; process until smooth. Pour into sieve set over bowl; press mixture with rubber spatula to extract all liquid. Discard pulp.** Return liquid to pan; whisk in sour cream until evenly blended. Add salt and white pepper to taste. Reheat but do not boil. Serve in individual bowls. Garnish with sunflower seeds.

Makes 4 servings

**May eliminate straining soup. Return processed soup to pan; whisk in sour cream. Proceed as above.

121

HEARTY soups & stews

New England Clam Chowder

24	medium fresh clams
	Salt
1	bottle (8 ounces) clam juice
3	medium potatoes, cut into ½-inch-thick slices
¼	teaspoon dried thyme leaves
¼	teaspoon white pepper
4	slices bacon, cut crosswise into ¼-inch strips
1	medium onion, chopped
⅓	cup all-purpose flour
2	cups milk
1	cup half-and-half
	Oyster crackers
	Fresh thyme for garnish

1. Scrub clams with stiff brush. Soak in mixture of ⅓ cup salt to 1 gallon water 20 minutes. Drain water; repeat 2 more times. Refrigerate clams 1 hour. Shuck clams, reserving juice. Strain clam juice through triple thickness of dampened cheesecloth; pour clam juice into 2-cup glass measure. Refrigerate until needed. Coarsely chop clams; set aside.

2. Add bottled clam juice and enough water to clam juice in glass measure to total 2 cups liquid; place liquid in Dutch oven. Add potatoes, thyme and pepper; bring to a boil. Reduce heat; simmer 15 minutes or until potatoes are tender, stirring occasionally. Meanwhile, cook bacon in medium skillet over medium heat until almost crisp. Add onion; cook until tender but not brown. Stir flour into bacon mixture. Whisk in milk; cook until mixture boils and thickens.

3. Add bacon mixture and half-and-half to potato mixture. Add clams and continue to heat until clams are firm. Serve with oyster crackers. Garnish, if desired.

Makes 6 main-dish servings

QuickTip

To shuck clams, take clam knife in one hand and a thick towel or glove in the other. Grip shell in palm of protected hand. Keeping shell level, insert tip of knife at seam near hinge; twist to pry shell until it snaps, using knife as leverage, but without forcing it. Twist to open shell, keeping level at all times to save liquor. Release the clam meat by scraping the bottom shell.

POZOLE BISQUE CHOWDER CHILI BOUILLABAISSE GUMBO PISTOU CIOPPIN

New England Clam Chowder

HEARTY soups & stews

Creamy Carrot Soup

3 cups water
4 cups sliced carrots
½ cup chopped onion
2 tablespoons packed brown sugar
2 teaspoons curry powder
2 cloves garlic, minced
⅛ teaspoon ground ginger
Dash ground cinnamon
½ chicken flavor bouillon cube
½ cup skim milk

In large saucepan, bring water to a boil. Add remaining ingredients except milk. Reduce heat to low; simmer 40 minutes or until carrots are tender. Remove from heat; pour mixture in batches into food processor or blender. Process until smooth. Return mixture to saucepan. Over low heat, stir in milk, heating until warm but not boiling. Serve warm.

Makes 6 servings

Favorite recipe from **The Sugar Association, Inc.**

Creamy Carrot Soup

2 tablespoons olive oil

1 onion, finely chopped

2 cups chicken broth

1 (9-ounce) package frozen artichoke hearts, thawed to room temperature

½ cup white wine

1 pound mixed shellfish (raw shrimp, peeled and deveined; raw scallops or canned crabmeat)

1 cup heavy or whipping cream

2 tablespoons chopped fresh parsley

1 teaspoon salt

½ teaspoon ground nutmeg

¼ teaspoon white pepper

"Dearhearts" Seafood Bisque

1. Heat oil in large skillet over medium-high heat. Add onion; cook and stir 5 minutes or until softened. Add chicken broth, artichokes and wine. Bring to a boil over medium-high heat. Reduce heat to low. Simmer, covered, 5 to 7 minutes.

2. Process soup in small batches in food processor or blender until smooth. Return soup to saucepan.

3. Stir in shellfish, cream, parsley, salt, nutmeg and pepper. Bring soup just to a simmer over medium heat. Reduce heat to low. Simmer very gently, uncovered, 5 to 10 minutes. *Do not boil.* (Shellfish will become tough if soup boils.) Garnish, if desired.

Makes 6 servings

Cream of Asparagus Soup

1	pound fresh asparagus
$3\frac{1}{2}$	cups chicken broth, divided
$\frac{1}{4}$	cup butter or margarine
$\frac{1}{4}$	cup all-purpose flour
$\frac{1}{2}$	cup light cream
$\frac{1}{2}$	teaspoon salt
$\frac{1}{8}$	teaspoon black pepper

Trim off coarse ends of asparagus. Cut asparagus into 1-inch pieces. Combine asparagus and 1 cup broth in medium saucepan; cook 12 to 15 minutes or until tender. Melt butter in large saucepan. Remove from heat; stir in flour. Gradually add remaining $2\frac{1}{2}$ cups broth; cook, stirring occasionally, until slightly thickened. Stir in cream, seasonings and cooked asparagus with liquid. Heat thoroughly.

Makes 6 to 8 servings

Note: Substitute 3 chicken bouillon cubes and $3\frac{1}{2}$ cups water for $3\frac{1}{2}$ cups chicken broth.

*Quick*Tip

When choosing asparagus, look for firm, straight stalks with closed, compact tips and even green shading. Never make the mistake of choosing a stalk based on its thickness.

127

HEARTY *soups & stews*

Wisconsin Sausage Soup

¹/₂ cup butter

1 onion, chopped

1 carrot, chopped

1 teaspoon minced garlic

1 cup all-purpose flour

2 cups chicken broth

2 cups milk

³/₄ cup beer

1 teaspoon Worcestershire sauce

¹/₂ teaspoon salt

¹/₂ teaspoon dry mustard

1 bay leaf

7 ounces Cheddar cheese, shredded

3 ounces Swiss cheese, shredded

¹/₂ pound HILLSHIRE FARM® Smoked Sausage

Melt butter in medium saucepan over medium heat. Add onion, carrot and garlic; sauté until softened. Add flour; cook 5 minutes, stirring often. Add chicken broth, milk, beer, Worcestershire sauce, salt, mustard and bay leaf. Reduce heat to low; cook until soup has thickened, whisking often.

Slowly whisk cheeses into soup until combined and smooth. Cut Smoked Sausage lengthwise into quarters, then slice into ¹/₂-inch pieces. Sauté sausage in small skillet over medium-high heat until heated through. Blot excess grease with paper towels; add sausage to soup. Remove bay leaf; serve soup hot.

Makes 8 to 10 servings

Wisconsin Sausage Soup

Country Cream of Chicken Chowder

¼	cup CRISCO® Oil
¼	cup finely chopped onion
¼	cup all-purpose flour
4	cups chicken broth
2	cups skim milk
1	bay leaf
3	cups frozen hash brown potatoes
1	package (10 ounces) frozen whole kernel corn
1	package (10 ounces) frozen cut green beans
1	package (10 ounces) frozen peas
1	package (10 ounces) frozen sliced carrots
1½	cups finely chopped cooked chicken
⅛	teaspoon pepper
2	tablespoons chopped fresh parsley *or* chives

1. Heat oil in large saucepan on medium heat. Add onion. Cook and stir until tender. Stir in flour. Cook until bubbly. Stir in broth and milk gradually. Cook and stir until mixture is bubbly and slightly thickened. Add bay leaf.

2. Add potatoes, corn, beans, peas and carrots. Increase heat to medium-high. Bring mixture back to a boil. Reduce heat to low. Simmer 5 minutes or until beans are tender. Stir in chicken and pepper. Heat thoroughly. Remove bay leaf. Serve sprinkled with parsley. *Makes 10 servings*

Curried Creamy Sweet Potato Soup

4 cups water

1 pound sweet potatoes, peeled and cut into 1-inch cubes

Nonstick cooking spray

1 tablespoon plus 1 teaspoon butter or margarine, divided

2 cups finely chopped yellow onions

2 cups fat-free (skim) milk, divided

3/4 teaspoon curry powder

1/2 teaspoon salt

Dash ground red pepper (optional)

Bring water to a boil in large saucepan over high heat. Add potatoes; return to a boil. Reduce heat to medium-low and simmer, uncovered, 15 minutes or until potatoes are tender.

Meanwhile, heat medium nonstick skillet over medium-high heat until hot. Coat with cooking spray; add 1 teaspoon butter and tilt skillet to coat bottom. Add onions; cook 8 minutes or until tender and golden.

Drain potatoes; place in blender with onions, 1 cup milk, curry powder, salt and ground red pepper, if desired. Blend until completely smooth. Return potato mixture to saucepan and stir in remaining 1 cup milk. Cook 5 minutes over medium-high heat or until heated through. Remove from heat and stir in remaining 1 tablespoon butter.

Makes 3 cups (3/4 cup per appetizer serving)

131

HEARTY soups & stews

HEARTY soups & stews

2 tablespoons butter or margarine

¾ cup chopped carrot

½ cup sliced celery

½ cup chopped onion

2 to 3 tablespoons flour

1 teaspoon dried thyme or Italian seasoning

1 can (17 ounces) cream-style corn

2 cups milk

1 can (12 ounces) STARKIST® Solid White Tuna, drained and chunked

1 cup water

1 teaspoon chicken flavor instant bouillon

Albacore Corn Chowder

In medium saucepan, melt butter over medium heat; sauté carrot, celery and onion about 3 minutes. Add flour and thyme; blend well. Cook 3 more minutes. Add corn, milk, tuna, water and bouillon, stirring to blend. Cover and simmer (do not boil) 5 minutes to heat through, stirring occasionally.

Makes 4 servings

Prep Time: 20 minutes

FoodFact

Tuna is not a single breed but the name given to a vast number of similar tasting fish that like to swim in both the Mediterranean and the Pacific. Sizes range from the enormous bluefin, which weighs up to 1600 pounds, to the can-bound albacore, which weighs in at 6 to 15 pounds.

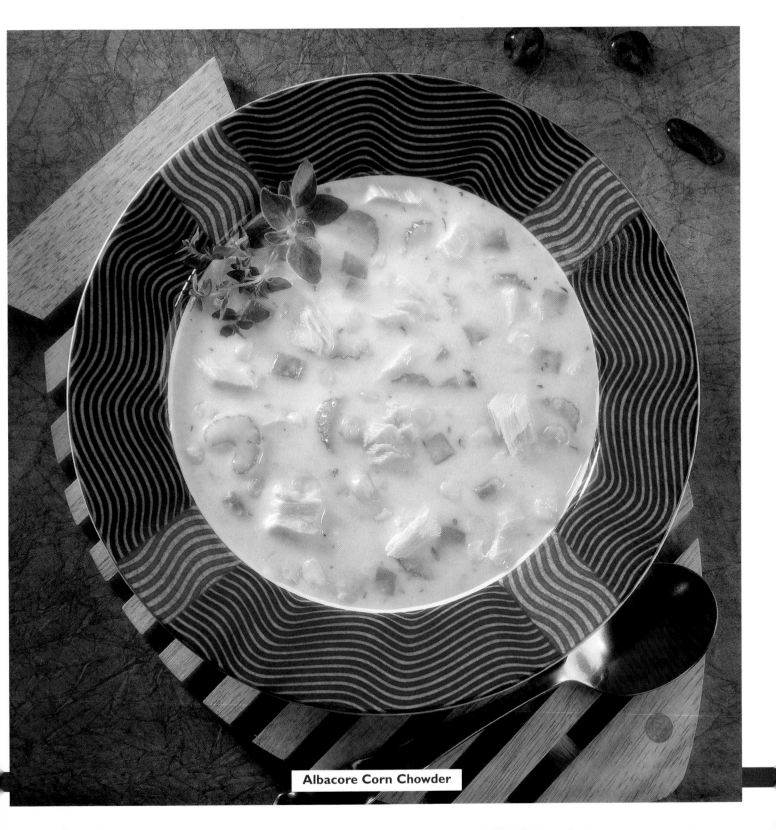

Albacore Corn Chowder

1 package (about 5 ounces) dry
   au gratin potatoes

1 can (about 15 ounces) whole
   kernel corn, undrained

2 cups water

1 cup salsa

2 cups milk

1½ cups (6 ounces) SARGENTO®
   Taco Blend Shredded Cheese

1 can (about 2 ounces) sliced ripe
   olives, drained

   Tortilla chips (optional)

Nacho Cheese Soup

In large saucepan, combine potatoes, dry au gratin sauce mix, corn with liquid, water and salsa. Heat to a boil; reduce heat. Cover and simmer 25 minutes or until potatoes are tender, stirring occasionally. Add milk, cheese and olives. Cook until cheese is melted and soup is heated through, stirring occasionally. Garnish with tortilla chips.   *Makes 6 servings*

*Food*Fact

A tortilla is a round, thin unleavened Mexican bread that is baked on a griddle. It can be made of either corn or wheat flour, water and a little salt. Traditionally the dough is shaped and flattened by hand and cooked on both sides on a hot griddle until dry and flecked with brown.

Nacho Cheese Soup

Cheddar Potato Chowder

3	tablespoons margarine or butter
2	medium-size carrots, peeled and diced
2	medium-size celery stalks, thinly sliced
1	small onion, chopped
3	tablespoons all-purpose flour
1/4	teaspoon dry mustard
1/4	teaspoon paprika
1/4	teaspoon ground pepper
2	cups milk
2	cups water
4	medium-size Idaho Potatoes (about 1¾ pounds), peeled and cut into ½-inch cubes
2	chicken-flavor bouillon cubes or envelopes
1½	cups shredded Cheddar cheese
4	slices bacon, cooked and crumbled (optional)
	Chopped chives (optional)

In 3-quart saucepan over medium heat, melt margarine. Add carrots, celery and onion; cook until tender, about 10 minutes, stirring occasionally. Stir in flour, dry mustard, paprika and pepper; cook 1 minute.

Gradually add milk, water, potatoes and bouillon. Bring to a boil over high heat; reduce heat to low. Cover and simmer 10 minutes or until potatoes are tender.

Remove saucepan from heat; add cheese and stir just until melted. Top each serving with crumbled bacon and chopped chives, if desired.   *Makes 4 servings*

*Favorite recipe from **Idaho Potato Commission***

Creamy Turkey Soup

2 cans (10½ ounces each) cream of chicken soup

2 cups chopped cooked turkey breast meat

1 package (8 ounces) sliced mushrooms

1 medium yellow onion, chopped

1 teaspoon rubbed sage *or* ½ teaspoon dried poultry seasoning

1 cup frozen peas, thawed

½ cup milk

1 jar (about 4 ounces) diced pimiento

Combine soup, turkey, mushrooms, onion and sage in slow cooker. Cook on LOW 8 hours or on HIGH 4 hours.

If cooking on LOW, turn to HIGH after 8 hours; stir in peas, milk and pimientos. Cook 10 more minutes or until heated through. *Makes 5 to 6 servings*

137

HEARTY *soups & stews*

Swiss Orzo Chowder

1¼	cups canned fat-free low-sodium chicken broth
1	cup frozen cut green beans
½	cup shredded carrot
⅓	cup (2 ounces) orzo or rosamarina
1	teaspoon dried basil leaves, crushed
¼	teaspoon black pepper
½	cup sliced yellow summer squash or zucchini
2½	cups fat-free skim milk, divided
3	tablespoons all-purpose flour
¼	cup shredded low-fat Swiss cheese

Combine broth, green beans, carrot, orzo, basil and pepper in medium saucepan. Bring to a boil over high heat; reduce heat to medium-low. Cover; simmer 10 minutes. Add squash. Cover; simmer about 2 minutes or until vegetables are tender.

Mix ½ cup milk and flour together in small bowl until smooth. Stir into vegetable mixture. Stir in remaining 2 cups milk. Cook and stir over medium heat until mixture boils and thickens. Cook and stir 1 minute more. Stir in Swiss cheese; heat until melted. *Makes 4 servings*

FoodFact

The word "orzo" actually means barley, even though the shape of this pasta looks more like rice. It is available in the pasta sections of large supermarkets.

Swiss Orzo Chowder

2 teaspoons CRICSO® Oil

¼ cup chopped green or red bell pepper

¼ cup chopped onion

2 tablespoons all-purpose flour

½ teaspoon dry mustard

⅛ teaspoon cayenne pepper

1 cup chicken broth

½ cup skim milk

1 package (10 ounces) mixed vegetables (broccoli, cauliflower and carrots) in cheese flavor sauce, thawed

1 package (9 ounces) frozen cut green beans, thawed

½ teaspoon salt

Cheesy Vegetable Soup

1. Heat oil in large saucepan on medium heat. Add green pepper and onion. Cook and stir 2 to 3 minutes or until crisp-tender. Remove from heat.

2. Stir in flour, dry mustard and cayenne. Stir in broth and milk gradually. Return to heat; cook and stir until mixture thickens.

3. Stir in vegetables in cheese sauce and green beans. Add salt. Simmer 5 minutes or until vegetables are tender.

Makes 4 servings

Creamy Crab Chowder

1 tablespoon butter or margarine

1 cup finely chopped onions

2 cloves garlic, minced

1 cup finely chopped celery

$\frac{1}{2}$ cup finely chopped green bell pepper

$\frac{1}{2}$ cup finely chopped red bell pepper

3 cans (13$\frac{3}{4}$ ounces each) chicken broth

3 cups peeled, diced potatoes

1 package (10 ounces) frozen corn

2 cans (6$\frac{1}{2}$ ounces each) lump crabmeat

$\frac{1}{4}$ teaspoon black pepper

$\frac{1}{2}$ cup half-and-half

Melt butter over medium heat in Dutch oven. Add onions and garlic. Cook and stir 6 minutes or until softened but not browned. Add celery and peppers. Cook 8 minutes or until celery is softened, stirring often.

Add broth and potatoes. Bring to a boil over high heat. Reduce heat to low and simmer 10 minutes. Add corn; cook 5 minutes or until potatoes are tender. Drain crabmeat and place in small bowl. Flake to break up large pieces. Add to Dutch oven. Stir in black pepper and half-and-half. Bring to a simmer. (Do not boil.) Serve hot. *Makes 6 to 8 servings*

141

HEARTY *soups & stews*

1/4 cup butter or margarine

1 pound medium raw shrimp, peeled, deveined and coarsely chopped into 1/2-inch pieces

2 large green onions, sliced

1 large clove garlic, minced

1/4 cup all-purpose flour

1 cup fish stock or canned chicken broth

3 cups half-and-half

1/2 teaspoon salt

1/2 teaspoon grated lemon peel

Dash ground red pepper

2 tablespoons white wine (optional)

Lemon peel twists and sliced green onion tops for garnish

Whole shrimp for garnish

Shrimp Bisque

1. Melt butter in large saucepan over medium heat. Cook and stir shrimp, onions and garlic in butter until shrimp turns pink and opaque. Remove from heat.

2. Blend in flour. Cook and stir just until bubbly. Stir in fish stock and cook until bubbly. Cook 2 minutes, stirring constantly. Remove from heat.

3. Process soup in small batches in food processor or blender until smooth. Return soup to saucepan.

4. Stir in half-and-half, salt, lemon peel, red pepper and wine, if desired; heat through. Garnish, if desired.

Makes 4 servings

Shrimp Bisque

¼ cup (½ stick) butter

½ cup minced onion

½ cup flour

¼ teaspoon baking soda

1¼ teaspoons salt

¼ teaspoon paprika

2½ cups milk

2½ cups bouillon or broth

½ cup diced carrots

½ cup diced celery

¼ pound sharp Wisconsin Cheddar cheese, cubed

1 tablespoon chopped parsley

Wisconsin Cheese Vegetable Soup

In large saucepan, melt butter. Sauté onion lightly. Add flour, baking soda and seasonings; blend well. Slowly add milk and bouillon to butter-flour mixture, stirring constantly to make smooth white sauce. Add vegetables and cheese cubes.

Simmer 15 minutes or until vegetables are tender and cheese is melted. Do not boil. (If soup boils, it may curdle.) Serve topped with parsley. *Makes 6 servings*

Favorite recipe from **Wisconsin Milk Marketing Board**

*Quick*Tip

To chop fresh parsley the no-mess way, place parsley sprigs in 1-cup measuring cup; snip with kitchen scissors until finely chopped.

Spinach and Mushroom Soup

1½ cups 1% milk

3 medium potatoes, peeled and chopped (1 cup)

1 box (10 ounces) BIRDS EYE® frozen Chopped Spinach

1 can (10¾ ounces) cream of mushroom soup

• In large saucepan, heat milk and potatoes over medium-low heat 10 minutes.

• Add spinach and soup.

• Cook about 10 minutes or until soup begins to bubble and potatoes are tender, stirring frequently. *Makes 4 servings*

Prep Time: 5 minutes
Cook Time: 20 minutes

Potato and Albacore Chowder

145

2 tablespoons butter or margarine

¼ cup chopped onion

¼ cup chopped celery

1 cup chopped or grated cooked potato

1 can (10¾ ounces) cream of potato soup

⅔ cup milk or half & half

⅔ cup chicken broth

1 (3-ounce) pouch of STARKIST® Solid White Tuna, drained and chunked

Freshly ground black pepper

Shredded Cheddar cheese

Snipped chives

In medium saucepan, melt butter over medium heat. Sauté onion and celery until onion is tender. Add potatoes; continue cooking 2 to 3 minutes. Add soup, milk, chicken broth and tuna; heat thoroughly over low heat. Top each serving with pepper, cheese and chives. *Makes 2 servings*

Prep Time: 10 minutes

HEARTY soups & stews

*Considered by some cultures to be a powerful **aphrodisiac**, beans are a popular and **nourishing** food. Give a few bean soups a whirl and who knows, maybe they'll do more than **dazzle** your taste buds.*

1   pound spicy Italian sausage, casing removed and sliced ½-inch thick

½   onion, chopped

2   cups frozen O'Brien-style potatoes with onions and peppers

1   can (15 ounces) pinto beans, undrained

¾   cup water

1   teaspoon beef bouillon granules *or* 1 beef bouillon cube

1   teaspoon dried oregano leaves

⅛   teaspoon ground red pepper

Skillet Sausage and Bean Stew

1. Combine sausage slices and onion in large nonstick skillet; cook and stir over medium-high heat 5 to 7 minutes or until meat is no longer pink. Drain drippings.

2. Stir in potatoes, beans, water, bouillon, oregano and red pepper; reduce heat to medium. Cover and simmer 15 minutes, stirring occasionally.   *Makes 4 servings*

Lighten Up: You can reduce the calories and fat content of this dish by substituting turkey sausage for Italian sausage. Add hot pepper sauce to taste if you prefer a spicier stew.

Prep and Cook Time: 30 minutes

Skillet Sausage and Bean Stew

2 cans (14½ ounces *each*) chicken broth *plus* water to equal 4 cups

1 can (14½ ounces) ready-cut Italian-style tomatoes, undrained

1 can (15¼ ounces) kidney beans, drained

¼ cup tomato paste

1 teaspoon Italian herb seasoning

½ teaspoon salt

⅛ teaspoon ground red pepper

½ cup uncooked small shell pasta

2 cups Italian-style frozen vegetables (zucchini, carrots, cauliflower, Italian green beans, lima beans)

1 can (12 ounces) STARKIST® Solid White Tuna, drained and chunked

3 cups fresh romaine lettuce, cut crosswise into 1-inch strips

Freshly grated Parmesan cheese

Tuna Minestrone with Parmesan Cheese

In 4-quart saucepan, combine chicken broth mixture, tomatoes with liquid, kidney beans, tomato paste, herb seasoning, salt and red pepper; bring to a boil over high heat. Add pasta and frozen vegetables; simmer 8 minutes. Remove from heat; add tuna and romaine. Serve with cheese.

Makes 6 to 8 servings

Prep Time: 10 minutes

*Quick*Tip

There are two basic kinds of canned broth: condensed (which requires an addition of water or milk) and ready to serve (which is single strength). Be careful not to use condensed broth, unless specifically called for in the recipe, or your soup will be too salty.

Tuna Minestrone with Parmesan Cheese

Spicy Lentil and Pasta Soup

2 medium onions, thinly sliced

$^1/_2$ cup chopped carrot

$^1/_2$ cup chopped celery

$^1/_2$ cup peeled and chopped turnip

1 small jalapeño pepper,* finely chopped

2 cans (about 14 ounces each) vegetable broth

1 can (14$^1/_2$ ounces) no-salt-added stewed tomatoes

2 cups water

8 ounces dried lentils, sorted, rinsed and drained

2 teaspoons chili powder

$^1/_2$ teaspoon dried oregano

3 ounces uncooked whole wheat spaghetti, broken

$^1/_4$ cup minced fresh cilantro

Jalapeño peppers can sting and irritate the skin; wear rubber gloves when handling peppers and do not touch eyes. Wash hands after handling.

1. Spray large nonstick saucepan with nonstick cooking spray; heat over medium heat until hot. Add onions, carrot, celery, turnip and jalapeño; cook and stir 10 minutes or until vegetables are crisp-tender.

2. Add vegetable broth, tomatoes, water, lentils, chili powder and oregano; bring to a boil. Reduce heat; simmer, covered, 20 to 30 minutes or until lentils are tender.

3. Add pasta; cook 10 minutes or until tender.

4. Ladle soup into bowls; sprinkle with cilantro.

Makes 6 servings

Spicy Lentil and Pasta Soup

1¼ cups dried navy beans

6 cups cold water

3 slices bacon, finely chopped

1 large onion, chopped

1 large rib celery, chopped

¾ pound smoked pork rib or neck bones

2 medium cloves garlic, minced

½ teaspoon dried thyme leaves, crushed

½ teaspoon dried marjoram leaves, crushed

¼ teaspoon black pepper

¾ cup uncooked small pasta shells

2 tablespoons chopped fresh parsley

Salt

1 cup beef broth (optional)

Freshly grated Parmesan cheese (optional)

Carrot flowers and fresh parsley for garnish

Pasta and Bean Soup

1. Rinse beans thoroughly in colander under cold running water, picking out any debris or blemished beans. Combine beans and water in large saucepan. To quick-soak beans, cover and bring to a boil over high heat; uncover and boil 2 minutes. Remove from heat; cover and let stand 1 hour. Do not drain.

2. Cook bacon in medium skillet over medium-high heat 2 minutes. Add onion and celery; cook and stir 6 minutes or until golden brown. Remove bacon, onion and celery with slotted spoon to plate; discard drippings.

3. Rinse bones; add to beans and soaking water. Add bacon mixture; stir in garlic, thyme, marjoram and pepper. Bring to boil over high heat; reduce heat to medium-low. Simmer 1 hour or until beans are tender, stirring occasionally. Remove from heat.

4. Remove bones to plate; set aside. Remove half of bean mixture with slotted spoon; place in food processor or blender. Add 2 tablespoons soup liquid; process until smooth.

5. Stir puréed bean mixture into soup. Bring soup to a boil over high heat. Stir in pasta. Reduce heat to medium-low; simmer, uncovered, 10 minutes or until pasta is tender, stirring occasionally. Meanwhile, remove meat from reserved bones; discard bones. Chop meat.

6. To serve, stir meat and parsley into soup. Season soup with salt to taste. If soup is too thick, add some beef broth. Serve with cheese. Garnish, if desired.   *Makes 6 servings*

Pasta and Bean Soup

3 cups low sodium chicken broth, defatted

1 jar (16 ounces) GUILTLESS GOURMET® Black Bean Dip (Spicy or Mild)

1 can (6 ounces) crabmeat, drained

2 tablespoons brandy (optional)

6 tablespoons low fat sour cream

Chopped fresh chives (optional)

Black Bean Bisque with Crab

Microwave Directions

Combine broth and bean dip in 2-quart glass measure or microwave-safe casserole. Cover with vented plastic wrap or lid; microwave on HIGH (100% power) 6 minutes or until soup starts to bubble.

Stir in crabmeat and brandy, if desired; microwave on MEDIUM (50% power) 2 minutes or to desired serving temperature. To serve, ladle bisque into 8 individual ramekins or soup bowls, dividing evenly. Swirl 1 tablespoon sour cream into each serving. Garnish with chives, if desired.

Makes 8 servings

*Quick*Tip

To prepare this dish on the stovetop, combine broth and bean dip in a 2-quart saucepan; bring to a boil over medium heat. Stir in crabmeat and brandy, if desired; cook 2 minutes or to desired serving temperature. Serve as directed.

Navy Bean and Ham Soup

1	bag (16 ounces) navy beans
1	tablespoon vegetable oil
$1/2$	cup chopped onion
$1/2$	cup chopped celery
1	pound ham, diced
2	cups water
1	can ($14^1/2$ ounces) chicken broth
2	bay leaves
$2^1/2$	teaspoons LAWRY'S® Seasoned Salt
2	teaspoons LAWRY'S® Garlic Powder with Parsley
$3/4$	teaspoon LAWRY'S® Seasoned Pepper

Wash beans and soak overnight, or for at least 4 hours. Pour off water from beans and rinse thoroughly. In soup pot or Dutch oven, heat oil. Add onion and celery and cook over medium-high heat until just tender. To pot, add drained beans and remaining ingredients. Bring to a boil over medium-high heat; reduce heat to low, cover and simmer 1 hour. Remove bay leaves and serve. *Makes 4 to 6 servings*

Serving Suggestion: Stir well and serve in individual bowls. Garnish with chopped green onion, if desired.

*Quick*Tip

For extra flavor, ham hocks can replace diced ham. Cook at least $1^1/2$ hours if hocks are used.

155

HEARTY soups & stews

Hearty Minestrone

1 cup dried pinto beans

2 teaspoons olive oil

½ cup chopped red onion

1 clove garlic, minced

3 cans (10 ounces each) no-salt-added whole tomatoes, undrained, chopped

1 medium potato, cut into ½-inch cubes

1 cup coarsely chopped carrots

1 cup thinly sliced zucchini

4 ounces coarsely shredded cabbage

⅔ cup coarsely chopped leek

½ cup coarsely chopped celery

2 cups no-salt-added vegetable juice cocktail

2 cups water

1 tablespoon chopped fresh basil

1 teaspoon chopped fresh sage

2 bay leaves

¼ teaspoon black pepper

1 cup small shell pasta

4 tablespoons freshly grated Parmesan cheese

1 tablespoon chopped fresh parsley

1. Place dried pinto beans in large glass bowl; cover completely with water. Soak 6 to 8 hours or overnight. Drain beans; discard water.

2. Heat oil in large heavy saucepan or Dutch oven over medium heat. Add onion and garlic; cook and stir until onion is tender.

3. Drain tomatoes, reserving liquid. Add tomatoes to saucepan; mix well. Add pinto beans, potato, carrots, zucchini, cabbage, leek and celery. Stir in vegetable juice, water and reserved tomato liquid. Add basil, sage, bay leaves and black pepper. Bring to a boil over high heat; reduce heat. Cover and simmer 2 hours, stirring occasionally.

4. Add pasta to saucepan 15 minutes before serving. Cook, uncovered, until soup thickens. Remove bay leaves; discard. Top with Parmesan and parsley.

Makes 10 (1½-cup) servings

Hearty Minestrone

Zesty Lentil Stew

1   cup dried lentils

2   cups chopped peeled potatoes

1   can (14½ ounces) reduced-sodium chicken broth, defatted

1⅔   cups water

1½   cups chopped seeded tomatoes

1   can (11½ ounces) no-salt-added spicy vegetable juice cocktail

1   cup chopped onion

½   cup chopped carrot

½   cup chopped celery

2   tablespoons chopped fresh basil *or* 2 teaspoons dried basil leaves, crushed

2   tablespoons chopped fresh oregano *or* 2 teaspoons dried oregano leaves, crushed

1   to 2 tablespoons finely chopped jalapeño pepper*

¼   teaspoon salt

Jalapeño peppers can sting and irritate the skin; wear rubber gloves when handling peppers and do not touch eyes. Wash hands after handling peppers.

Rinse lentils under cold water; drain. Combine lentils, potatoes, broth, water, tomatoes, vegetable juice cocktail, onion, carrot, celery, basil, oregano, jalapeño pepper and salt in 3-quart saucepan.

Bring to a boil over high heat. Reduce heat to medium-low. Cover; simmer 45 to 50 minutes or until lentils are tender, stirring occasionally.   *Makes 4 servings*

*Quick*Tip

Lentils are a healthful, meatless meal choice. They are a good source of calcium, iron, vitamins A and B and phosphorus. Vegetarians should substitute vegetable broth for the chicken broth to suit vegetarian diets.

Zesty Lentil Stew

6 strips (about 6 ounces) bacon, cut into ½-inch pieces

3 cans (15 ounces each) white beans, drained, rinsed and divided

3 cans (about 14 ounces each) reduced-sodium chicken broth

1 medium onion, finely chopped

3 cloves garlic, minced

1½ teaspoons dried thyme leaves

1½ teaspoons dried rosemary

White Bean Soup

1. Cook and stir bacon in Dutch oven over medium-high heat about 10 minutes or until crisp.

2. While bacon is cooking, blend 1½ cans beans and broth in blender or food processor until smooth.

3. Drain all but 1 tablespoon bacon fat from Dutch oven. Stir in onion, garlic, thyme and rosemary. Reduce heat to medium; cover and cook 3 minutes or until onion is transparent. Uncover and cook 3 minutes or until onion is tender, stirring frequently.

4. Add puréed bean mixture and remaining 1½ cans beans to bacon mixture. Cover and simmer 5 minutes or until heated through. *Makes 4 servings*

Prep and Cook Time: 28 minutes

Quick Tip

Cannellini, Great Northern and navy are varieties of white beans that can be used in this soup. For a special touch, sprinkle chopped fresh thyme over the soup just before serving.

Sopa De Sonora

1 tablespoon salad oil

1 pound boneless lean pork shoulder, trimmed and cut into 1-inch cubes

1½ tablespoons LAWRY'S® Minced Onion with Green Onion Flakes

¼ teaspoon LAWRY'S® Garlic Powder with Parsley

1 package (1.48 ounces) LAWRY'S® Spices & Seasonings for Chili

4½ cups water

1 can (14½ ounces) beef broth

1 cup dried pinto beans, rinsed

2 cups thinly sliced carrots

LAWRY'S® Seasoned Salt to taste

Condiments:

Cherry tomatoes, cut into fourths

Sliced green onion

Chopped cilantro

Lime wedges

Dairy sour cream

LAWRY'S® Chunky Taco Sauce

In Dutch oven, heat oil. Add pork and cook over medium-high heat until browned. Add remaining ingredients, except carrots, Seasoned Salt and condiments; mix well. Bring to a boil over medium-high heat; reduce heat to low, cover and simmer 1½ hours. Add carrots, cover and simmer about 30 minutes or until carrots are tender. Add Seasoned Salt to taste.

Makes 6 to 8 servings

Serving Suggestion: Serve with condiments.

161

HEARTY soups & stews

QuickTip

Use beef bouillon and water rather than beef broth, if desired; just follow the package directions for bouillon proportions. Use 1 pound boneless beef chuck roast instead of pork, if desired.

Spicy African Chick-Pea and Sweet Potato Stew

Spice Paste

6	cloves garlic, peeled
1	teaspoon coarse salt
2	teaspoons sweet paprika
1½	teaspoons cumin seeds
1	teaspoon cracked black pepper
½	teaspoon ground ginger
½	teaspoon ground allspice
1	tablespoon olive oil

Stew

1½	pounds sweet potatoes, peeled and cubed
2	cups canned vegetable broth or water
1	can (16 ounces) plum tomatoes, undrained, chopped
1½	cups sliced fresh okra *or* 1 package (10 ounces) frozen cut okra, thawed
1	can (16 ounces) chick-peas, drained and rinsed
	Yellow Couscous (recipe follows)
	Hot pepper sauce
	Fresh cilantro for garnish

1. Process garlic and salt in blender or small food processor until garlic is finely chopped. Add paprika, cumin, black pepper, ginger and allspice; process 15 seconds. While blender is running, pour oil through cover opening; process until paste forms. Set Spice Paste aside.

2. Combine sweet potatoes, broth, tomatoes with juice, okra, chick-peas and Spice Paste in large saucepan. Bring to boil over high heat. Reduce heat to low. Cover and simmer 15 minutes. Uncover; simmer 10 minutes or until vegetables are tender.

3. Prepare Yellow Couscous. Serve stew with couscous and red pepper sauce. Garnish, if desired. *Makes 4 servings*

Yellow Couscous

1	tablespoon olive oil
5	green onions, sliced
1⅔	cups water
¼	teaspoon salt
⅛	teaspoon saffron threads *or* ½ teaspoon ground turmeric
1	cup precooked couscous*

Check ingredient label for "precooked semolina."

Heat oil in medium saucepan over medium heat until hot. Add onions; cook and stir 4 minutes. Add water, salt and saffron. Bring to a boil. Stir in couscous. Remove from heat. Cover; let stand 5 minutes. *Makes 3 cups*

Spicy African Chick-Pea and Sweet Potato Stew

Rustic Vegetable Soup

1   jar (16 ounces) picante sauce

1   package (10 ounces) frozen
    mixed vegetables, thawed

1   package (10 ounces) frozen cut
    green beans, thawed

1   can (10 ounces) condensed beef
    broth, undiluted

1   to 2 baking potatoes, cut into
    $\frac{1}{2}$-inch pieces

1   medium green bell pepper,
    chopped

$\frac{1}{2}$ teaspoon sugar

$\frac{1}{4}$ cup finely chopped parsley

Combine picante sauce, mixed vegetables, green beans, beef broth, potatoes, bell pepper and sugar in slow cooker. Cover and cook on LOW 8 hours or on HIGH 4 hours. Stir in parsley; serve.

Makes 8 servings

Rustic Vegetable Soup

Spiced Carrot, Lentil and Coriander Soup

3   tablespoons FILIPPO BERIO®
    Olive Oil

1   large onion, sliced

1   pound carrots, sliced

8   ounces dried red or brown
    lentils (about 1¼ cups),
    rinsed and drained

2   teaspoons ground coriander

2   teaspoons ground cumin

6   cups chicken broth

2   cups milk

    Salt and freshly ground black
    pepper

    Fresh cilantro sprigs (optional)

In large saucepan, heat olive oil over medium heat until hot. Add onion and carrots; cook and stir 5 minutes. Add lentils, coriander and cumin; cook and stir 1 minute. Stir in chicken broth; bring to a boil. Cover; reduce heat to low and simmer 30 minutes or until lentils and carrots are tender. Cool slightly.

Process soup in small batches in blender or food processor until smooth. Return soup to saucepan; stir in milk. Heat through. Season to taste with salt and pepper. Garnish with cilantro, if desired. Serve hot.   *Makes 6 to 8 servings*

*Food*Fact

Coriander is the plant whose leaves are referred to as cilantro. Ground coriander comes from the plant's seeds, which have a very different flavor—similar to a combination of lemon, sage and caraway—from that of the leaves.

Black-Eyed Pea Soup

2 large potatoes

4 medium onions, thinly sliced

4 carrots, thinly sliced

½ pound bacon, diced

8 quarts water

2 pounds dried black-eyed peas, rinsed

2 cups thinly sliced celery

1 meaty ham bone

2 whole jalapeño peppers*

4 bay leaves

½ teaspoon dried thyme leaves, crushed

Salt and black pepper to taste

*Jalapeño peppers can sting and irritate the skin; wear rubber gloves when handling peppers and do not touch eyes. Wash hands after handling.

1. Peel and grate potatoes. Place in large bowl of cold water; set aside.

2. Combine onions, carrots and bacon in large stockpot. Cook and stir over medium-high heat until onions are golden.

3. Drain potatoes. Add water, black-eyed peas, potatoes, celery, ham bone, jalapeño peppers, bay leaves and thyme to onion mixture. Season with salt and black pepper. Reduce heat to low. Simmer, covered, 3 to 4 hours. Remove and discard jalapeño peppers and bay leaves.

4. Remove ham bone; cool. Cut meat from bone; chop meat into bite-size pieces. Return to stockpot.

Makes 12 to 16 servings

HEARTY *soups & stews*

Spicy Lentil and Chick-Pea Soup

$^{1}/_{2}$ cup dried chick-peas (garbanzo beans)

4 cans (14 ounces each) reduced-sodium chicken broth

1 cup dried lentils

1 large onion, chopped

1 rib celery, chopped

1 teaspoon ground turmeric

$^{1}/_{2}$ teaspoon salt

$^{1}/_{2}$ teaspoon ground cinnamon

$^{1}/_{2}$ teaspoon black pepper

$^{1}/_{4}$ teaspoon ground ginger

$^{1}/_{4}$ teaspoon ground red pepper

3 cups chopped ripe tomatoes

$^{1}/_{4}$ cup uncooked rice

$^{1}/_{4}$ cup chopped fresh parsley

2 tablespoons chopped fresh cilantro

6 lemon wedges

1. Sort and rinse chick-peas; place in large saucepan. Cover with water and let soak overnight; drain chick-peas and return to saucepan. Add chicken broth to saucepan; bring to a boil over high heat. Reduce heat to low; cover and simmer 1 hour.

2. Sort and rinse lentils; add to chick-peas with onion, celery, turmeric, salt, cinnamon, black pepper, ginger and ground red pepper. Cover and simmer 45 minutes or until lentils are tender.

3. Stir in tomatoes and rice; bring to a boil over medium-high heat. Reduce heat to low; cover and simmer 20 to 25 minutes or until rice is tender.

4. Stir in parsley and cilantro; simmer 5 minutes. Serve with lemon wedges; garnish with additional fresh cilantro, if desired.

Makes 6 servings

Spicy Lentil and Chick-Pea Soup

1 (14½-ounce) can HUNT'S®
  Choice-Cut Diced Tomatoes
  with Roasted Garlic,
  undrained

2 (14½-ounce) cans low fat and
  low sodium chicken broth

1 (15-ounce) can black beans,
  rinsed and drained

1 cup frozen whole kernel corn

1 teaspoon oregano leaves,
  crushed

¼ teaspoon ground cumin

6 ounces fully cooked reduced fat
  smoked turkey sausage, halved
  lengthwise and thinly sliced

Turkey and Black Bean Soup

1. In medium saucepan combine Hunt's Choice-Cut Diced Tomatoes and *remaining* ingredients *except* sausage.

2. Bring to a boil. Reduce heat; simmer, uncovered, for 3 minutes.

3. Stir in sausage; heat through.

Makes 6 (1-cup) servings

Rosarita Refried Soup

WESSON® No-Stick Cooking
   Spray

1   cup diced onion

1   (16-ounce) can ROSARITA®
    Traditional No-Fat Refried
    Beans

6   cups fat free, low sodium
    chicken broth

1   (14½-ounce) can HUNT'S®
    Choice-Cut Diced Tomatoes

4   cups baked tortilla chips

½   cup shredded reduced fat
    Monterey Jack cheese

¼   cup chopped fresh cilantro

1. Spray a large saucepan with Wesson Cooking Spray. Sauté onion over low heat for 5 minutes.

2. Add Rosarita Beans, broth and Hunt's Tomatoes; mix well. Cook until heated through.

3. Place ½ cup tortilla chips in each bowl. Ladle soup into bowls. Garnish with cheese and cilantro.

Makes 12 (1-cup) servings

*Food*Fact

Refried beans are served at almost every meal in Mexico. Despite their name, they are only fried once. The confusion is a result of an imperfect translation of "frijoles refritos," which implies that the beans should be thoroughly fried after the preliminary cooking.

171

HEARTY *soups & stews*

Vegetable Soup with Delicious Dumplings

Soup

Soup

2	tablespoons WESSON® Vegetable Oil
1	cup diced onion
3/4	cup sliced celery
7	cups homemade chicken broth *or* 4 (14½-ounce) cans chicken broth
2	(14½-ounce) cans HUNT'S® Stewed Tomatoes
½	teaspoon garlic powder
½	teaspoon salt
½	teaspoon fines herbes seasoning
⅛	teaspoon pepper
1	(16-ounce) bag frozen mixed vegetables
1	(15½-ounce) can HUNT'S® Red Kidney Beans, drained
⅓	cup uncooked long-grain rice

Dumplings

2	cups all-purpose flour
3	tablespoons baking powder
1	teaspoon salt
⅔	cup milk
⅓	cup WESSON® Vegetable Oil
1½	teaspoons chopped fresh parsley

Soup

In a large Dutch oven, heat Wesson Oil. Add onion and celery; sauté until crisp-tender. Stir in *next 6 ingredients*, ending with pepper; bring to a boil. Add vegetables, beans and rice. Reduce heat; cover and simmer 15 to 20 minutes or until rice is cooked and vegetables are tender.

Dumplings

Meanwhile, in a medium bowl, combine flour, baking powder and salt; blend well. Add milk, Wesson Oil and parsley; mix until batter forms a ball in the bowl. Drop dough by rounded tablespoons into simmering soup. Cook, covered, 10 minutes; remove lid and cook an additional 10 minutes.

Makes 10 servings

QuickTip

Fines herbes seasoning mixture typically contains chervil, chive, parsley and tarragon.

Vegetable Soup with Delicious Dumplings

2   tablespoons FILIPPO BERIO®
    Olive Oil

2   medium potatoes, peeled and
    quartered

2   medium onions, sliced

3   cups beef broth

8   ounces fresh green beans,
    trimmed and cut into
    1-inch pieces

3   carrots, peeled and chopped

8   ounces fresh spinach, washed,
    drained, stemmed and
    chopped

1   green bell pepper, diced

2   tablespoons chopped fresh
    parsley

1   tablespoon chopped fresh basil
    or 1 teaspoon dried basil
    leaves

½   teaspoon ground cumin

1   clove garlic, finely minced

    Salt and freshly ground black
    pepper

Vegetable Soup

In Dutch oven, heat olive oil over medium-high heat until hot. Add potatoes and onions; cook and stir 5 minutes. Add beef broth, green beans and carrots. Bring mixture to a boil. Cover; reduce heat to low and simmer 10 minutes, stirring occasionally. Add spinach, bell pepper, parsley, basil, cumin and garlic. Cover; simmer an additional 15 to 20 minutes or until potatoes are tender. Season to taste with salt and black pepper. Serve hot.   *Makes 6 to 8 servings*

*Quick*Tip

Olive oil should be stored in a cool, dark place for up to 6 months. It can be refrigerated as well, in which case it will last up to a year. Since oil will become too thick to pour when cold, let it reach room temperature and become liquid again before using.

Vegetable Soup

³/₄	cup uncooked brown rice
¹/₂	cup dry lentils, rinsed
¹/₂	cup chopped onion
¹/₂	cup sliced celery
¹/₂	cup sliced carrots
¹/₄	cup chopped parsley
1	teaspoon Italian herb seasonings
1	clove garlic, minced
1	bay leaf
2¹/₂	cups chicken broth
2	cups water
1	can (14¹/₂ ounces) tomatoes, chopped, undrained
1	tablespoon cider vinegar

Brown Rice and Lentil Stew

Combine rice, lentils, onion, celery, carrots, parsley, Italian herb seasonings, garlic, bay leaf, broth, water, tomatoes and vinegar in Dutch oven. Bring to a boil over high heat. Reduce heat to low. Simmer, uncovered, about 1 hour or until rice is tender, stirring occasionally. Remove bay leaf before serving.

Makes 4 servings

Favorite recipe from **USA Rice Federation**

*Quick*Tip

Brown rice contains the bran and germ of the rice kernel, making it more nutritious than white rice. Brown rice also takes longer to cook, proving that good things come to those who wait.

White Bean and Green Chile Pepper Soup

2 cans (15 ounces each) Great Northern beans, rinsed and drained

1 cup finely chopped yellow onion

1 can (4½ ounces) diced green chilies

1 teaspoon ground cumin, divided

½ teaspoon garlic powder

1 can (14½ ounces) fat-free chicken broth

¼ cup chopped fresh cilantro leaves

1 tablespoon extra virgin olive oil

⅓ cup sour cream (optional)

1. Combine beans, onion, chilies, ½ teaspoon cumin and garlic powder in slow cooker. Cook on LOW 8 hours or on HIGH 4 hours.

2. Stir in cilantro, olive oil and remaining ½ teaspoon cumin. Garnish with sour cream, if desired.   *Makes 5 servings*

177

HEARTY soups & stews

1½ cups dried baby lima beans

1 teaspoon olive oil

½ cup chopped celery

⅓ cup coarsely chopped onion

2 cloves garlic, minced

2 cans (10 ounces each) no-salt-added whole tomatoes, undrained, chopped

½ cup chopped fresh parsley

2 tablespoons fresh rosemary

¼ teaspoon black pepper

3 cups shredded fresh escarole

White Bean and Escarole Soup

1. Place dried lima beans in large glass bowl; cover completely with water. Soak 6 to 8 hours or overnight. Drain beans; place in large saucepan or Dutch oven. Cover beans with about 3 cups water; bring to a boil over high heat. Reduce heat to low. Cover and simmer about 1 hour or until soft. Drain; set aside.

2. Heat oil in small skillet over medium heat. Add celery, onion and garlic; cook until onion is tender. Remove from heat.

3. Add celery mixture and tomatoes with juice to beans. Stir in parsley, rosemary and black pepper. Cover and simmer over low heat 15 minutes. Add escarole; simmer 5 minutes.

Makes 6 (1½-cup) servings

QuickTip

Escarole, curly endive and Belgian endive are the three main varieties of endive. Escarole has the mildest flavor and smoother, broader, pale-green leaves. It is available year-round, but is most plentiful from June to October.

White Bean and Escarole Soup

2   tablespoons vegetable oil

3   green onions, minced

3   cloves garlic, finely minced

4   cans (16 ounces each) red
    kidney beans, undrained

2   cans (14½ ounces each) beef
    broth

⅓   cup *Frank's® RedHot®* Cayenne
    Pepper Sauce

¼   cup minced fresh cilantro

2   teaspoons ground cumin

1   teaspoon dried oregano leaves

Baja Red Bean Soup

1. Heat oil in 5-quart saucepan. Add onions and garlic; cook 3 minutes or until tender. Add beans with liquid, broth, **Frank's RedHot** Sauce, cilantro, cumin and oregano. Bring to a boil, stirring occasionally. Reduce heat; simmer, partially covered, 30 minutes, stirring occasionally.

2. Remove 2 cups soup. Place in blender; cover securely and process until smooth. Return to saucepan; stir. Cook until heated through. Garnish with sour cream and shredded Cheddar cheese, if desired.   *Makes 10 servings*

Prep Time: 15 minutes
Cook Time: 35 minutes

*Quick*Tip

This soup freezes well. Freeze leftovers in individual portions. Thaw and reheat in a microwave oven.

Lentil Soup

1 tablespoon FILIPPO BERIO®
   Olive Oil

1 medium onion, diced

4 cups beef broth

1 cup dried lentils, rinsed and
   drained

¼ cup tomato sauce

1 teaspoon dried Italian herb
   seasoning

   Salt and freshly ground black
   pepper

In large saucepan, heat olive oil over medium heat until hot. Add onion; cook and stir 5 minutes or until softened. Add beef broth; bring mixture to a boil. Stir in lentils, tomato sauce and Italian seasoning. Cover; reduce heat to low and simmer 45 minutes or until lentils are tender. Season to taste with salt and pepper. Serve hot.   *Makes 6 servings*

Picante Black Bean Soup

4 slices bacon

1 large onion, chopped

1 clove garlic, minced

2 cans (15 ounces each) black
   beans, undrained

1 can (about 14 ounces) beef
   broth

1¼ cups water

¾ cup PACE® Picante Sauce

½ to 1 teaspoon salt

½ teaspoon dried oregano leaves,
   crushed

   Sour cream

   Crackers and additional PACE®
   Picante Sauce for serving

1. Using scissors, cut bacon into ½×½-inch pieces.

2. Cook and stir bacon in large saucepan over medium-high heat until crisp. Remove with slotted spoon; drain on paper towels. Set bacon aside.

3. Add onion and garlic to drippings in saucepan; cook and stir 3 minutes. Add beans with liquid, broth, water, ¾ cup picante sauce, salt and oregano. Reduce heat to low. Simmer, covered, 20 minutes.

4. Ladle into soup bowls; dollop with sour cream. Sprinkle with bacon. Serve with crackers and additional picante sauce.
Makes 6 to 8 servings

181

HEARTY *soups & stews*

*Warm up from the **inside out** on a chilly winter day. Get out of that parka and snuggle up to a **bowlful** of your favorite hearty **warmup**.*

Potato Soup with Green Chilies & Cheese

2	tablespoons vegetable oil
1	medium onion, chopped
1	clove garlic, minced
2	cups chopped unpeeled potatoes
1	tablespoon all-purpose flour
1½	cups chicken broth
2	cups milk
1	can (4 ounces) diced green chilies
½	teaspoon celery salt
¾	cup (3 ounces) shredded Monterey Jack cheese
¾	cup (3 ounces) shredded Colby or Cheddar cheese
	White pepper
	Chopped celery leaves for garnish

Heat oil in 3-quart pan over medium heat. Add onion and garlic; cook until onion is tender. Stir in potatoes; cook 1 minute. Stir in flour; continue cooking 1 minute. Stir in broth. Bring to a boil. Cover; reduce heat and simmer 20 minutes or until potatoes are tender. Stir in milk, chilies and celery salt; heat to simmering. Add cheeses; stir and heat just until cheeses melt. Do not boil. Add pepper to taste. Serve in individual bowls. Garnish with celery leaves.

Makes 6 servings

Potato Soup with Green Chilies & Cheese

Hot Gazpacho Bean Soup

1	tablespoon olive oil
1	cup chopped onion
1	cup chopped green bell pepper
1	clove garlic, minced
2	cans (11½ ounces each) no-salt-added vegetable juice
1	can (15 ounces) red kidney beans, rinsed and drained
1	can (15 ounces) garbanzo beans, rinsed and drained
2	beef bouillon cubes
2	tablespoons fresh lemon juice
¼	teaspoon red pepper flakes
3	cups chopped tomatoes, divided
1	cup chopped cucumber
½	cup chopped green onions
½	cup plain salad croutons

1. Heat olive oil in medium saucepan over medium-high heat until hot. Add onion, green pepper and garlic. Cook 3 minutes or until vegetables are crisp-tender.

2. Add vegetable juice, beans, bouillon cubes, lemon juice, red pepper flakes and 1½ cups tomatoes. Bring to a boil. Reduce heat to low. Cover and simmer 5 minutes.

3. Divide bean mixture among serving bowls. Top with remaining tomatoes, cucumber, green onions and croutons.

Makes 6 servings

Prep and Cook Time: 28 minutes

*Food*Fact

Traditionally, gazpacho is a cold, uncooked purée of fresh tomatoes, onions, garlic, bell peppers, cucumber and olive oil, among other ingredients. This version includes beans, for those who like to break from tradition, and calls for cooking the soup, for those who like it hot.

Hot Gazpacho Bean Soup

186

1 tablespoon BERTOLLI® Olive Oil

1 chicken (3 to 3½ pounds), cut
   into serving pieces (with or
   without skin)

4 large carrots, cut into 2-inch
   pieces

3 ribs celery, cut into 1-inch pieces

1 large onion, cut into 1-inch
   wedges

1 envelope LIPTON® RECIPE
   SECRETS® Savory Herb with
   Garlic Soup Mix*

1½ cups water

½ cup apple juice

Parsley Dumplings, optional
   (recipe follows)

*Also terrific with Lipton® Recipe Secrets® Golden
Onion Soup Mix.*

Country Chicken Stew with Dumplings

In 6-quart Dutch oven or heavy saucepot, heat oil over medium-high heat and brown ½ of the chicken; remove and set aside. Repeat with remaining chicken. Return chicken to Dutch oven. Stir in carrots, celery, onion and savory herb with garlic soup mix blended with water and apple juice. Bring to a boil over high heat. Reduce heat to low and simmer covered 25 minutes or until chicken is done and vegetables are tender.

Meanwhile, prepare Parsley Dumplings. Drop 12 rounded tablespoonfuls of batter into simmering broth around chicken. Continue simmering, covered, 10 minutes or until toothpick inserted in center of dumpling comes out clean. Season stew, if desired, with salt and pepper.

Makes about 6 servings

Parsley Dumplings: In medium bowl, combine 1⅓ cups all-purpose flour, 2 teaspoons baking powder, 1 tablespoon chopped fresh parsley and ½ teaspoon salt; set aside. In measuring cup, blend ⅔ cup milk, 2 tablespoons melted butter or margarine and 1 egg. Stir milk mixture into flour mixture just until blended.

Country Chicken Stew with Dumplings

Golden Tomato Soup

4   teaspoons reduced-calorie
     margarine
1   cup chopped onion
2   cloves garlic, coarsely chopped
½   cup chopped carrot
¼   cup chopped celery
8   medium Florida tomatoes,
     blanched, peeled, seeded and
     chopped
6   cups chicken broth
¼   cup uncooked rice
2   tablespoons tomato paste
1   tablespoon Worcestershire sauce
½   teaspoon dried thyme leaves,
     crushed
¼   to ½ teaspoon ground black
     pepper
5   drops hot pepper sauce

Melt margarine in large Dutch oven over medium-high heat. Add onion and garlic; cook and stir 1 to 2 minutes or until onion is tender. Add carrot and celery; cook and stir 7 to 9 minutes or until tender, stirring frequently. Stir in tomatoes, broth, rice, tomato paste, Worcestershire sauce, thyme, black pepper and hot pepper sauce. Reduce heat to low; cook about 30 minutes, stirring frequently.

Remove from heat. Let cool about 10 minutes. In food processor or blender, process soup in small batches until smooth. Return soup to Dutch oven; simmer 3 to 5 minutes or until heated through. Garnish as desired.

Makes 8 servings

Favorite recipe from **Florida Tomato Committee**

QuickTip

To blanch and peel tomatoes, place them one at a time in a saucepan of simmering water for about 10 seconds. (Add about 30 seconds if they are not fully ripened.) Then immediately plunge them into a bowl of cold water for another 10 seconds. The skins will peel off easily with a knife. Do not add more than one tomato at a time to the water or the temperature will drop rapidly and the tomatoes will stew before their skins can be removed.

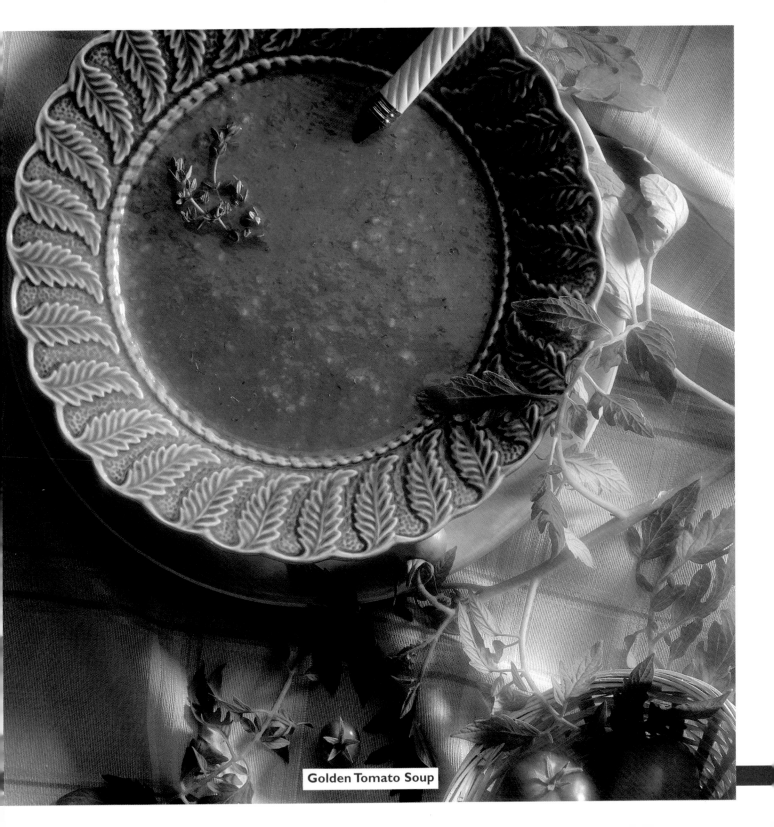

Golden Tomato Soup

190

4 medium onions, chopped

2 tablespoons butter or margarine

1 can (14½ ounces) DEL MONTE® Diced Tomatoes

1 can (10½ ounces) condensed beef consommé

¼ cup dry sherry

4 French bread slices, toasted

1½ cups (6 ounces) shredded Swiss cheese

¼ cup (1 ounce) grated Parmesan cheese

Tomato French Onion Soup

1. Cook onions in butter in large saucepan about 10 minutes. Add undrained tomatoes, 2 cups water, consommé and sherry to saucepan. Bring to boil, skimming off foam.

2. Reduce heat to medium-low; simmer 10 minutes. Place soup in four broilerproof bowls; top with bread and cheeses. Broil until cheeses are melted and golden.

Makes 4 servings

Prep and Cook Time: 35 minutes

QuickTip

If broilerproof bowls are not available, place soup in ovenproof bowls and bake at 350°F 10 minutes.

Tomato French Onion Soup

1 pound carrots, peeled and
   chopped

1 medium onion, chopped

1 tablespoon margarine

4 cups chicken broth, divided

¼ teaspoon dried tarragon leaves

¼ teaspoon ground white pepper

2¼ cups cooked rice

¼ cup light sour cream

Snipped parsley or mint for
garnish

Carrot-Rice Soup

Cook carrots and onion in margarine in large saucepan or Dutch oven over medium-high heat 2 to 3 minutes or until onion is tender. Add 2 cups broth, tarragon, and pepper. Reduce heat; simmer 10 minutes. Combine vegetables and broth in food processor or blender; process until smooth. Return to saucepan. Add remaining 2 cups broth and rice; thoroughly heat. Dollop sour cream on each serving of soup. Garnish with parsley. *Makes 6 servings*

Favorite recipe from **USA Rice Federation**

Ham and Beer Cheese Soup

1 cup chopped onion

½ cup sliced celery

2 tablespoons butter or margarine

1 cup hot water

1 HERB-OX® chicken flavor bouillon cube *or* 1 teaspoon instant chicken bouillon

3 cups half-and-half

3 cups (18 ounces) diced CURE 81® ham

1 (16-ounce) loaf pasteurized process cheese spread, cubed

1 (12-ounce) can beer

3 tablespoons all-purpose flour

Popcorn (optional)

In Dutch oven over medium-high heat, sauté onion and celery in butter until tender. In small liquid measuring cup, combine water and bouillon to make broth; set aside. Add half-and-half, ham, cheese, beer and ¾ cup broth to onion and celery mixture. Cook, stirring constantly, until cheese melts. Combine remaining ¼ cup broth and flour; stir until smooth. Add flour mixture to soup, stirring constantly. Cook, stirring constantly, until slightly thickened. Sprinkle individual servings with popcorn, if desired. *Makes 8 servings*

193

HEARTY *soups & stews*

1   tablespoon canola oil

1   onion, sliced

3   cloves garlic, minced

2   teaspoons red pepper flakes

2   teaspoons dried oregano leaves, crushed

1   teaspoon ground cumin

1   can (28 ounces) tomatoes, chopped

1   can (15 ounces) chick-peas (garbanzo beans), rinsed and drained

1   can (15 ounces) pinto beans, rinsed and drained

2   cups whole kernel corn, fresh or frozen

1   cup water

6   cups shredded iceberg lettuce

Mexican Hot Pot

1. Heat oil in stockpot or Dutch oven over medium-high heat. Add onion and garlic; cook and stir 5 minutes. Add red pepper flakes, oregano and cumin; mix well.

2. Stir in tomatoes, chick-peas, pinto beans, corn and water; bring to a boil over high heat.

3. Reduce heat to medium-low; cover and simmer 15 minutes. Top individual servings with 1 cup shredded lettuce. Serve hot.   *Makes 6 servings*

Mexican Hot Pot

1 cup chopped celery

¹/₂ cup thinly sliced leek (white part only)

¹/₂ cup chopped carrot

¹/₂ cup chopped turnip

6 cups fat-free reduced-sodium chicken broth, divided

1 tablespoon minced fresh parsley

1¹/₂ teaspoons fresh thyme *or* ¹/₂ teaspoon dried thyme leaves

1 teaspoon fresh rosemary *or* ¹/₄ teaspoon dried rosemary

1 teaspoon balsamic vinegar

¹/₄ teaspoon black pepper

2 ounces uncooked yolk-free wide noodles

1 cup diced cooked chicken breast

Vegetable-Chicken Noodle Soup

1. Place celery, leek, carrot, turnip and ¹/₃ cup chicken broth in large saucepan. Cover; cook over medium heat until vegetables are tender, stirring occasionally.

2. Stir in remaining chicken broth, parsley, thyme, rosemary, vinegar and pepper. Bring to a boil; add noodles. Cook until noodles are tender; stir in chicken. Reduce heat to medium. Simmer until heated through.   *Makes 6 servings*

*Quick*Tip

Since this recipe combines two of the most nostalgic soups—vegetable and chicken noodle—it just might be the ultimate comfort food.

Vegetable-Chicken Noodle Soup

Harvest Soup

½ pound BOB EVANS® Special
   Seasonings Roll Sausage

1 large onion, finely chopped

2½ cups chicken broth

2 cups canned pumpkin

2 cups hot milk

1 teaspoon lemon juice

   Dash ground nutmeg

   Dash ground cinnamon

   Salt and black pepper to taste

   Chopped fresh parsley

Crumble and cook sausage and onion in large saucepan until sausage is browned. Drain off any drippings. Add broth and bring to a boil. Stir in pumpkin; cover and simmer over low heat 15 to 20 minutes. Add milk, lemon juice, nutmeg, cinnamon, salt and pepper; simmer, uncovered, 5 minutes to blend flavors. Sprinkle with parsley before serving. Refrigerate leftovers.

Makes 6 to 8 servings

Shrimp & Sausage Gumbo

1 tablespoon vegetable oil

1 large onion, chopped

2 ribs celery, chopped

2 cloves garlic, minced

1/2 pound sweet Italian sausage, casings removed

1 can (14 1/2 ounces) tomatoes, cut up, undrained

3 tablespoons *Frank's® RedHot®* Cayenne Pepper Sauce

2 teaspoons minced fresh thyme *or* 1 teaspoon dried thyme leaves

1 bay leaf

1 package (10 ounces) frozen cut okra, thawed and drained

1/2 pound raw large shrimp, shelled and deveined

Cooked white rice (optional)

1. Heat oil in large nonstick skillet over medium-high heat. Add onion, celery and garlic; cook until tender. Add sausage; cook until no longer pink, stirring to separate meat. Drain well.

2. Add tomatoes with liquid, **Frank's RedHot** Sauce, thyme and bay leaf. Bring to a boil. Reduce heat to low; cook, covered, 10 minutes.

3. Stir in okra and shrimp; cook, covered, 3 minutes or until okra is tender and shrimp turn pink. Remove and discard bay leaf. Serve over rice, if desired. *Makes 4 servings*

Prep Time: 20 minutes
Cook Time: 23 minutes

199

HEARTY *soups & stews*

Cajun-Style Chicken Soup

1½   pounds chicken thighs

4   cups chicken broth

1   can (8 ounces) tomato sauce

2   ribs celery, sliced

1   medium onion, chopped

2   cloves garlic, minced

2   bay leaves

1   to 1½ teaspoons salt

½   teaspoon ground cumin

¼   teaspoon paprika

¼   teaspoon ground red pepper

¼   teaspoon black pepper

   Dash white pepper

1   large green bell pepper, chopped

⅓   cup uncooked rice

8   ounces fresh or frozen okra, cut into ½-inch slices

   Hot pepper sauce (optional)

   Fresh oregano for garnish

Place chicken, chicken broth, tomato sauce, celery, onion, garlic, bay leaves, salt, cumin, paprika, red pepper, black pepper and white pepper in 5-quart Dutch oven. Bring to a boil over high heat. Reduce heat to medium-low; simmer, uncovered, 1 hour or until chicken is tender, skimming foam that rises to the surface.

Remove chicken from soup; cool slightly. Skim fat from soup. Remove chicken meat from bones; discard skin and bones. Cut chicken into bite-size pieces.

Add chicken, bell pepper and rice to soup. Bring to a boil. Reduce heat; simmer, uncovered, about 12 minutes or until rice is tender. Add okra; simmer an additional 8 minutes or until okra is tender. Discard bay leaves. Ladle soup into bowls; serve with hot pepper sauce. Garnish, if desired.

Makes 6 servings

Cajun-Style Chicken Soup

Brunswick Stew

2 pounds chicken pieces, rinsed

2¹⁄₃ cups cold water, divided

1 can (14¹⁄₂ ounces) tomatoes, cut up and undrained

2 large ribs celery, sliced

1 medium onion, chopped

2 cloves garlic, minced

1 bay leaf

¹⁄₂ teaspoon salt

¹⁄₈ teaspoon ground red pepper

6 small unpeeled new potatoes (about ³⁄₄ pound), cut in half

1 cup frozen succotash (about ¹⁄₂ of 10-ounce package)

1 cup cubed ham

1 tablespoon all-purpose flour

1. Combine chicken, 2 cups cold water, tomatoes with juice, celery, onion, garlic, bay leaf, salt and red pepper in 5-quart Dutch oven. Bring to a boil over high heat. Reduce heat to medium-low; simmer, uncovered, 45 minutes or until chicken is tender, skimming foam that rises to top.

2. Remove chicken from broth; cool slightly. Discard bay leaf. Skim fat from soup. Remove chicken meat from bones; discard skin and bones. Cut chicken into bite-size pieces.

3. Add potatoes, succotash and ham to Dutch oven. Bring to a boil. Reduce heat; simmer, uncovered, 20 minutes or until potatoes are tender. Stir in chicken. Stir flour into remaining ¹⁄₃ cup cold water until smooth. Stir into stew. Cook and gently stir over medium heat until bubbly.

Makes 6 servings

*Quick*Tip

Succotash is a mixture of corn and lima beans and is available in your grocery's freezer section.

Brunswick Stew

6 tablespoons butter or margarine, divided

1 small onion, finely chopped

4 cups water, divided

3 teaspoons instant chicken bouillon granules

8 ounces fresh assorted exotic mushrooms, such as cepes, shiitake, oyster, portobello, crimini, morels or chanterelles *or* 8 ounces button mushrooms, sliced

1 teaspoon lemon juice

4 tablespoons all-purpose flour

1/4 teaspoon white pepper

1 cup half-and-half or heavy cream

Exotic Mushroom Soup

1. Heat 2 tablespoons butter in 2-quart saucepan over medium-high heat until melted and bubbly. Cook and stir onion in hot butter until soft. Add 3½ cups water and bouillon; cover. Bring mixture to a boil over high heat; reduce heat to medium-low.

2. If using shiitake, chanterelle or morel mushrooms, slice stems and caps; add to broth mixture. Slice other types of mushroom stems thinly and add to broth mixture; reserve caps. Simmer broth mixture 10 minutes.

3. Slice reserved mushroom caps. Heat 2 tablespoons butter in medium skillet over medium-high heat until melted and bubbly. Cook and stir mushrooms briefly in hot butter until softened. Remove with slotted spoon to broth mixture.

4. Melt remaining 2 tablespoons butter with lemon juice in same skillet. Stir in flour and pepper, then remaining ½ cup water; blend well. Add to broth mixture and blend in with wire whisk. Cook until mixture thickens, stirring constantly. Stir in half-and-half.

5. Ladle into 6 bowls. Garnish, if desired.

Makes 6 appetizer servings

QuickTip

If using button mushrooms, slice them lengthwise through caps and stems; add them to broth mixture.

POZOLE BISQUE CHOWDER CHILI BOUILLABAISSE GUMBO PISTOU CIOPPIN

Exotic Mushroom Soup

Veggie Soup

1   bag (16 ounces) BIRDS EYE® frozen Mixed Vegetables

1   can (11 ounces) tomato rice soup

1   can (10 ounces) French onion soup

1   soup can of water

• In large saucepan, cook vegetables according to package directions; drain.

• Add both cans of soup and water; cook over medium-high heat until heated through.   *Makes 4 servings*

Serving Suggestion: Sprinkle individual servings evenly with 1 cup shredded Cheddar cheese.

Prep Time: 2 minutes
Cook Time: 10 to 12 minutes

Chicken Rotini Soup

½   pound boneless skinless chicken breasts, cut into ½-inch pieces

1   cup water

2   tablespoons butter or margarine

4   ounces fresh mushrooms, sliced

½   medium onion, chopped

4   cups chicken broth

1   teaspoon Worcestershire sauce

¼   teaspoon dried tarragon leaves, crushed

¾   cup uncooked rotini

1   small zucchini

    Fresh basil for garnish

Combine chicken and water in medium saucepan. Bring to a boil over high heat. Reduce heat to medium-low; simmer 2 minutes. Drain water and rinse chicken. Melt butter in 5-quart Dutch oven or large saucepan over medium heat. Add mushrooms and onion. Cook and stir until onion is tender. Stir in chicken, chicken broth, Worcestershire and tarragon. Bring to a boil over high heat. Stir in uncooked pasta. Reduce heat to medium-low; simmer, uncovered, 5 minutes. Cut zucchini into ⅛-inch slices; halve any large slices. Add to soup; simmer, uncovered, about 5 minutes, or until pasta is tender. Ladle into bowls. Garnish, if desired.
Makes 4 servings

Veggie Soup

4 ounces fresh spinach, washed

3 carrots, peeled

6 cups fish stock or chicken broth

4 green onions, sliced

2 tablespoons chopped fresh dill

2 teaspoons white wine Worcestershire sauce

2 teaspoons lemon juice

1 pound bay scallops, rinsed and patted dry

Salt and white pepper to taste

Scallops & Mock Seaweed Soup

1. To cut spinach into chiffonade strips, make "V-shaped" cut at stem end. Roll up leaf jelly-roll fashion. Slice crosswise into 1/2-inch-thick slices with chef's knife. Repeat with remaining leaves; set aside.

2. To cut carrot decoratively, use citrus stripper or grapefruit spoon to cut groove into carrot, cutting lengthwise from stem end to tip. Continue to cut grooves about 1/4 inch apart until completely around carrot. Thinly slice crosswise. Repeat with remaining carrots.

3. Bring fish stock to a simmer in large saucepan; add carrot slices to stock. Bring to a boil; simmer 5 minutes or until carrots are crisp-tender.

4. Add spinach, green onions, dill, Worcestershire and lemon juice to soup; simmer 1 to 2 minutes.

5. Add scallops; simmer briefly until scallops turn opaque. Season with salt and pepper; serve immediately.

Makes 6 servings

Scallops & Mock Seaweed Soup

1   tablespoon olive or vegetable oil

1½   pounds stew meat

2   cups baby carrots

1   package (8 ounces) fresh mushrooms, sliced

2   cups (14½ ounces each) beef broth

1   can (14½ ounces) diced tomatoes

2   cups water

1   envelope LIPTON® RECIPE SECRETS® Onion Soup Mix

¾   cup barley

1   cup frozen peas

Hearty Beef Barley Stew

1. In 6-quart saucepot, heat oil over medium-high heat, brown beef, stirring occasionally, 4 minutes.

2. Stir in carrots, mushrooms, broth, tomatoes, water, soup mix and barley.

3. Bring to a boil over high heat. Reduce heat to medium-low and simmer, covered, 1½ hours, stirring occasionally. Stir in peas. Cook 5 minutes or until heated through.

Makes 6 servings

Prep Time: 10 minutes
Cook Time: 1 hour 40 minutes

*Quick*Tip

To prepare this stew in a slow cooker, layer carrots, mushrooms and beef in the slow cooker. Combine broth, tomatoes, water, soup mix and barley. Pour over the beef and vegetables. Cover and cook on HIGH 5 to 6 hours or LOW 8 to 10 hours. Stir in peas and cook until heated through, about 5 minutes. Season, if desired, with salt and pepper.

Roman Spinach Soup

6 cups reduced-sodium chicken broth

1 cup cholesterol-free egg substitute

¼ cup minced fresh basil

3 tablespoons freshly grated Parmesan cheese

2 tablespoons lemon juice

1 tablespoon minced fresh parsley

¼ teaspoon white pepper

⅛ teaspoon ground nutmeg

8 cups fresh spinach, washed, stems removed, chopped

1. Bring broth to a boil in large saucepan over medium heat.

2. Beat together egg substitute, basil, Parmesan cheese, lemon juice, parsley, white pepper and nutmeg in small bowl. Set aside.

3. Stir spinach into broth; simmer 1 minute. Slowly pour egg mixture into broth mixture, whisking constantly so egg threads form. Simmer 2 to 3 minutes or until egg is cooked. Garnish with lemon slices, if desired. Serve immediately.

Makes 8 (¾-cup) servings

Note: Soup may look curdled.

211

HEARTY *soups & stews*

2¼ cups water, divided

1 cup stone-ground or regular yellow cornmeal

2 eggs

2 egg whites

¾ cup reduced-fat sharp Cheddar cheese

1 jalapeño pepper,* minced

1 teaspoon margarine

½ teaspoon salt, divided

1 tablespoon olive oil

2 cups coarsely chopped and peeled eggplant

1 cup chopped onion

3 cloves minced garlic

3 cups chopped zucchini

1 cup chopped tomato

½ cup chopped yellow bell pepper

2 tablespoons minced fresh parsley

1 tablespoon minced fresh oregano

¼ teaspoon minced fresh rosemary

¼ teaspoon crushed red pepper

¼ teaspoon ground pepper blend

Jalapeño peppers can sting and irritate the skin; wear rubber gloves when handling peppers and do not touch your eyes. Wash hands after handling jalapeño peppers.

Cheesy Polenta with Zucchini Stew

1. Bring 2 cups water to a boil. Slowly stir in cornmeal. Bring to a boil, stirring constantly, until mixture thickens. Lightly beat eggs and egg whites with remaining ¼ cup water. Add to cornmeal; cook and stir until bubbly. Remove from heat; stir in cheese, jalapeño pepper, margarine and ¼ teaspoon salt. Pour into 9-inch square baking pan. Cover and refrigerate several hours or until firm.

2. Heat olive oil in medium saucepan over medium heat until hot. Cook and stir eggplant, onion and garlic 5 minutes or until onion is transparent. Add zucchini, tomato, bell pepper, parsley, oregano, rosemary, remaining ¼ teaspoon salt, red pepper and pepper blend. Simmer, uncovered, 1 hour.

3. Spray large nonstick skillet with nonstick vegetable cooking spray. Heat skillet over medium heat until hot. Cut polenta into 6 rectangles. Cook over medium heat 8 minutes on each side or until crusty and lightly browned. Serve zucchini stew over polenta. *Makes 6 servings*

Cheesy Polenta with Zucchini Stew

HEARTY soups & stews

214

- ¼ cup olive oil
- 4 carrots, chopped
- 1 onion, cut into quarters
- 1 cup chopped celery
- 2 cloves garlic, finely chopped
- 1 teaspoon finely chopped fennel
  Salt and black pepper to taste
- 12 small new potatoes
- 1 pound mushrooms, cut into halves
- 2 cans (12 ounces each) diced tomatoes, undrained
- 1 can (8 ounces) tomato sauce
- 1 tablespoon dried oregano leaves
- 1 pound HILLSHIRE FARM® Polska Kielbasa, sliced

Hearty Sausage Stew

Heat oil in heavy skillet over medium-high heat; add carrots, onion, celery, garlic, fennel, salt and pepper. Sauté until vegetables are soft. Add potatoes, mushrooms, tomatoes with liquid, tomato sauce and oregano; cook 20 minutes over low heat. Add Polska Kielbasa; simmer 15 minutes or until heated through.

Makes 6 servings

Quick Tip

If you don't have 2 cups of tomato sauce, you can substitute ¾ cup tomato paste mixed into 1 cup of water.

Hearty Sausage Stew

2 cans (about 14 ounces each) vegetable or chicken broth

2 teaspoons bottled minced garlic

1 teaspoon bottled minced fresh ginger *or* $\frac{1}{2}$ teaspoon ground ginger

$\frac{1}{4}$ teaspoon red pepper flakes

1 package (16 ounces) frozen vegetable medley, such as broccoli, carrots, water chestnuts and red bell peppers

1 package (5 ounces) Oriental curly noodles *or* 5 ounces angel hair pasta, broken in half

3 tablespoons soy sauce

1 tablespoon dark sesame oil

$\frac{1}{4}$ cup thinly sliced green onion tops

Szechuan Vegetable Lo Mein

1. Combine broth, garlic, ginger and red pepper flakes in large deep skillet. Cover and bring to a boil over high heat.

2. Add vegetables and noodles to skillet; cover and return to a boil. Reduce heat to medium-low; simmer, uncovered, 5 to 6 minutes or until noodles and vegetables are tender, stirring occasionally.

3. Stir soy sauce and sesame oil into broth mixture; cook 3 minutes. Stir in green onions; ladle into bowls.

Makes 4 servings

Prep and Cook Time: 20 minutes

Quick **Tip**

For a heartier, protein-packed main dish, add 1 package (10½ ounces) extra-firm tofu, cut into ¾-inch pieces, to the broth mixture with the soy sauce and sesame oil.

Szechuan Vegetable Lo Mein

6 ounces boneless skinless chicken breast, cut into ½-inch pieces

3½ teaspoons curry powder, divided

1 teaspoon olive oil

¾ cup chopped apple

½ cup sliced carrot

⅓ cup sliced celery

¼ teaspoon ground cloves

2 cans (about 14 ounces each) fat-free reduced-sodium chicken broth

½ cup orange juice

4 ounces uncooked radiatore pasta

Chicken Curry Soup

1. Coat chicken with 3 teaspoons curry powder. Heat oil in large saucepan over medium heat until hot. Add chicken; cook and stir 3 minutes or until no longer pink in center. Remove from pan; set aside.

2. Add apple, carrot, celery, remaining ½ teaspoon curry powder and cloves to same pan; cook, stirring occasionally, 5 minutes. Add chicken broth and juice; bring to a boil over high heat. Reduce heat to medium-low. Add pasta; cover. Cook, stirring occasionally, 8 to 10 minutes or until pasta is tender; add chicken. Remove from heat. Ladle into soup tureen or individual bowls. Top each serving with a dollop of plain nonfat yogurt, if desired. *Makes 4 (¾-cup) servings*

*Food*Fact

Curry powder is actually a blend of up to 20 different spices, herbs and seeds, including turmeric, cardamom, cumin, pepper, cloves, cinnamon, nutmeg, ginger, chilies and coriander.

Chicken Curry Soup

Butternut Bisque

1   teaspoon margarine or butter

1   large onion, coarsely chopped

1   medium butternut squash
    (about 1½ pounds), peeled,
    seeded and cut into ½-inch
    pieces

2   cans (about 14 ounces each)
    reduced-sodium or regular
    chicken broth, divided

½   teaspoon ground nutmeg or
    freshly grated nutmeg

⅛   teaspoon white pepper

    Plain nonfat yogurt and chives
    for garnish (optional)

Melt margarine in large saucepan over medium heat. Add onion; cook and stir 3 minutes.

Add squash and 1 can chicken broth; bring to a boil over high heat. Reduce heat to low; cover and simmer 20 minutes or until squash is very tender.

Process squash mixture, in 2 batches, in food processor until smooth. Return soup to saucepan; add remaining can of broth, nutmeg and pepper. Simmer, uncovered, 5 minutes, stirring occasionally.*

Ladle soup into soup bowls. Place yogurt in pastry bag fitted with round decorating tip. Pipe onto soup in decorative design. Garnish with chives, if desired.

Makes about 6 (5-cup) servings

At this point, soup may be covered and refrigerated up to 2 days before serving. Reheat over medium heat, stirring occasionally.

Cream of Butternut Soup: Add ½ cup whipping cream or half-and-half with second can of broth. Proceed as directed.

Butternut Bisque

Dublin Coddle

½ pound fresh Brussels sprouts

2 pounds potatoes, peeled and sliced ½-inch thick

1 pound Irish pork sausage,* sliced into 1-inch pieces

1 pound smoked ham, cut into cubes

½ pound fresh baby carrots

3 medium onions, cut into 1-inch pieces

1 teaspoon dried thyme leaves

½ teaspoon black pepper

Irish pork sausage is similar to fresh garlic-flavored bratwurst. If unavailable, substitute 1 pound regular pork sausage and add 1 clove minced garlic with other ingredients in step 4.

1. Cut stem from each Brussels sprout and pull off outer bruised leaves. Cut an "X" deep into stem end of each sprout with paring knife.

2. Place potatoes, sausage, ham, sprouts, carrots, onions, thyme and pepper in Dutch oven. Add enough water to just barely cover ingredients. Bring to a boil over high heat. Reduce heat to medium. Cover and simmer 20 minutes. Uncover; continue cooking 15 minutes or until vegetables are tender. Remove from heat.

3. Cool slightly. Skim any fat from surface of liquid by lightly pulling clean paper towel across surface, letting any fat absorb into paper. To serve, spoon meat and vegetables into individual bowls along with some of the broth.

Makes 8 to 10 servings

Quick Tip

Dublin Coddle is a favorite Saturday night dish in its namesake city. Coddle refers to the method of simmering, or "coddling" ingredients in water. Do as Dubliners do and wash this meal down with a pint of dark, strong beer, such as stout.

Dublin Coddle

4   cups thinly sliced green cabbage

1½   pounds fresh beets, shredded

5   small carrots, peeled, cut lengthwise into halves, then cut into 1-inch pieces

1   parsnip, peeled, halved and cut into 1-inch pieces

1   cup chopped onion

4   cloves garlic, minced

1   pound lean beef stew meat, cut into ½-inch cubes

1   can (14½ ounces) diced tomatoes, undrained

3   cans (about 14 ounces each) reduced-sodium beef broth

¼   cup lemon juice

1   tablespoon sugar

1   teaspoon black pepper

    Sour cream (optional)

    Fresh parsley (optional)

Russian Borscht

Slow Cooker Directions

Layer ingredients in slow cooker in the following order: cabbage, beets, carrots, parsnip, onion, garlic, beef, tomatoes with juice, broth, lemon juice, sugar and pepper. Cover and cook on LOW 7 to 9 hours or until vegetables are crisp-tender. Season with additional lemon juice and sugar, if desired. Dollop with sour cream and garnish with parsley, if desired.

Makes 12 servings

Russian Borscht

5 pounds COLORADO potatoes, peeled and cubed (about 15 cups)

3 large onions, finely chopped (about 1 pound)

3 tablespoons instant chicken bouillon granules

2 tablespoons dried marjoram leaves

1 tablespoon dry mustard

1 teaspoon ground black pepper

4 quarts milk, divided

1¼ cups all-purpose flour

1 pound process Swiss cheese, shredded

1½ pounds sodium-reduced ham, diced

½ cup snipped fresh parsley

Hearty Potato-Ham Chowder

Steam potatoes and onions in 1 quart water 20 to 30 minutes or until tender. *Do not drain.* Mash slightly. Stir in bouillon granules, marjoram, mustard and pepper. Combine about 1 quart milk with flour; whisk to blend until smooth. Add remaining milk, cheese and milk/flour mixture to potato mixture. Cook and stir over medium-high heat until slightly thickened and bubbly. Cook and stir 2 minutes longer. Stir in ham and parsley; return to near boiling. Reduce heat; serve hot.

Makes 24 servings

*Favorite recipe from **Colorado Potato Administrative Committee***

Hearty Potato-Ham Chowder

Sausage & Zucchini Soup

1   pound BOB EVANS® Italian Roll Sausage

1   medium onion, diced

1   (28-ounce) can stewed tomatoes

2   (14-ounce) cans beef broth

2   medium zucchini, diced or sliced (about 2 cups)

2   small carrots, diced

2   stalks celery, diced

4   large mushrooms, sliced

    Grated Parmesan cheese for garnish

Crumble and cook sausage and onion in large saucepan over medium heat until sausage is browned. Drain off any drippings. Add remaining ingredients except cheese; simmer, uncovered, over low heat about 40 minutes or until vegetables are tender. Garnish with cheese. Refrigerate leftovers.

Makes 8 servings

228

FoodFact

Zucchini is the most popular summer squash. Distinguished by their edible skins and seeds, summer squashes differ widely in skin color and shape. But the mild, delicate flavor found in all varieties makes them largely interchangeable in recipe use.

Sausage & Zucchini Soup

2   bags SUCCESS® Brown Rice

1   pound ground turkey

1   small onion, chopped

2   cans (14$\frac{1}{2}$ ounces each)
    tomatoes, cut up, undrained

1   teaspoon pepper

$\frac{1}{2}$ teaspoon dried basil leaves,
    crushed

$\frac{1}{2}$ teaspoon garlic powder

1   can (16 ounces) whole kernel
    corn, drained

Country Stew

Prepare rice according to package directions.

Brown ground turkey with onion in large skillet, stirring occasionally to separate turkey. Add tomatoes with juice, pepper, basil and garlic powder; simmer 20 minutes, stirring occasionally. Stir in rice and corn; heat thoroughly, stirring occasionally. Garnish, if desired.   *Makes 8 servings*

Wonton Soup

¼ pound ground pork, chicken or turkey

¼ cup finely chopped water chestnuts

2 tablespoons soy sauce, divided

1 egg white, slightly beaten

1 teaspoon minced fresh ginger

12 wonton wrappers

1 can (46 ounces) chicken broth

1½ cups sliced fresh spinach leaves

1 cup thinly sliced cooked pork (optional)

½ cup diagonally sliced green onions

1 tablespoon dark sesame oil

Shredded carrot for garnish

Combine ground pork, water chestnuts, 1 tablespoon soy sauce, egg white and ginger in small bowl; mix well. Place 1 wonton wrapper with a point toward edge of counter. Mound 1 teaspoon of filling toward bottom point. Fold bottom point over filling, then roll wrapper over once. Moisten inside points with water. Bring side points together below the filling, overlapping slightly; press together firmly to seal. Repeat with remaining wrappers and filling. Keep finished wontons covered with plastic wrap, while filling remaining wrappers.

Combine broth and remaining 1 tablespoon soy sauce in large saucepan. Bring to a boil over high heat. Reduce heat to medium; add wontons. Simmer, uncovered, 4 minutes. Stir in spinach, sliced pork and onions; remove from heat. Stir in sesame oil. Ladle into soup bowls. Garnish with shredded carrot.

Makes 2 servings

231

HEARTY *soups & stews*

OZOLE BISQU

CIOPPINO

1   teaspoon olive oil

$1/3$ cup minced onion

$1/3$ cup sliced carrot

3   cups sliced fresh mushrooms

1   teaspoon ground sage

$1/4$ teaspoon ground thyme

$1/4$ teaspoon black pepper

$1/4$ cup dry red wine

2   cans (about 14 ounces each) fat-free reduced-sodium beef broth

$1/4$ cup tomato paste

2   ounces uncooked small bow tie pasta

Buttons & Bows

1. Heat oil in large saucepan over medium heat until hot. Add onion and carrot; cook 2 minutes. Add mushrooms, sage, thyme and pepper; cook and stir 5 minutes or until mushrooms are soft. Add wine; cook 2 minutes or until wine is reduced by half. Add beef broth; bring to a boil over medium-high heat. Add tomato paste and pasta; cover. Cook, stirring occasionally, 10 to 12 minutes or until pasta is tender.

2. Ladle into soup tureen or individual bowls. Serve immediately.   *Makes 4 (³/₄-cup) servings*

Buttons & Bows

'Chow Time' Chili

*Looking for something to spice up the **chuck wagon?** Fire it up as **peppery hot** as you want with some ch-ch-ch-chili! Your little rodeo team will come running at **chow time.***

Chunky Vegetarian Chili

1   tablespoon vegetable oil

1   medium green bell pepper, chopped

1   medium onion, chopped

3   cloves garlic, minced

2   cans (14½ ounces each) Mexican-style tomatoes, undrained

1   can (15 ounces) kidney beans, rinsed and drained

1   can (15 ounces) pinto beans, rinsed and drained

1   can (11 ounces) whole-kernel corn, drained

2½   cups water

1   cup uncooked rice

2   tablespoons chili powder

1½   teaspoons ground cumin

Sour cream (optional)

Heat oil in 3-quart saucepan or Dutch oven over medium-high heat. Add bell pepper, onion and garlic and cook and stir 5 minutes or until tender. Add tomatoes, beans, corn, water, rice, chili powder and cumin; stir well. Bring to a boil. Reduce heat; cover. Simmer 30 minutes, stirring occasionally. To serve, top with sour cream, if desired.   *Makes 6 servings*

Favorite recipe from **USA Rice Federation**

Chunky Vegetarian Chili

Nonstick cooking spray

1   pound ground chicken

1½   cups coarsely chopped onions
      (about 2 medium)

3   cups coarsely chopped celery

3   cloves garlic, minced

4   teaspoons chili powder

1½   teaspoons ground cumin

¾   teaspoon ground allspice

¾   teaspoon ground cinnamon

½   teaspoon black pepper

1   can (16 ounces) whole tomatoes,
      undrained, coarsely chopped

1   can (15½ ounces) Great
      Northern beans, rinsed and
      drained

2   cups fat-free low-sodium chicken
      broth

White Bean Chili

1. **SPRAY** large nonstick skillet with cooking spray; heat over medium heat until hot. Add chicken; cook and stir until browned, breaking into pieces with fork. Remove chicken; drain fat from skillet.

2. **ADD** onions, celery and garlic to skillet; cook and stir over medium heat 5 to 7 minutes or until tender. Sprinkle with chili powder, cumin, allspice, cinnamon and pepper; cook and stir 1 minute.

3. **RETURN** chicken to skillet. Stir in tomatoes with juice, beans and chicken broth; heat to a boil. Reduce heat to low and simmer, uncovered, 15 minutes. Garnish as desired.

Makes 6 entrée servings

White Bean Chili

238

Three Bean Chili

$^2/_3$ cup dried kidney beans

$^2/_3$ cup dried navy beans

$^2/_3$ cup dried black beans

10 cups cold water, divided

3 medium carrots, sliced

1 medium onion, chopped

2 teaspoons chili powder

$^1/_2$ teaspoon ground cumin

1 bay leaf

1 teaspoon salt

1 fresh jalapeño pepper,* chopped

1 can (28 ounces) tomatoes, cut up, undrained

$^1/_3$ cup tomato paste (about $^1/_2$ of 6-ounce can)

　　Salt

2 cups hot cooked rice

　　Shredded Cheddar cheese, sour cream, diced onion (optional)

　　Fresh oregano and yellow bell pepper curls for garnish

*Jalapeño peppers can sting and irritate the skin; wear rubber gloves when handling peppers and do not touch eyes. Wash hands after handling.

1. Rinse dried beans thoroughly in colander under cold running water, picking out any debris or blemished beans.

2. Cover beans with 6 cups of water. Soak overnight.

3. Drain beans; discard water. Combine beans, remaining 4 cups water, carrots, onion, chili powder, cumin, bay leaf and 1 teaspoon salt in 5-quart Dutch oven. Bring to a boil over high heat. Reduce heat to medium-low; simmer, uncovered, 1½ hours, stirring occasionally.

4. Remove bay leaf. Stir jalapeño pepper, tomatoes and tomato paste into bean mixture. Bring to a boil over high heat. Reduce heat to medium-low; simmer, uncovered, 15 minutes, stirring occasionally. Season with salt to taste.

5. Ladle chili over mounds of cooked rice in bowls. Serve with shredded Cheddar cheese, sour cream and diced onion, if desired. Garnish, if desired.　　　*Makes 6 servings*

Three Bean Chili

5   dried ancho chilies

2   cups water

2   tablespoons lard or vegetable oil

1   large onion, chopped

2   cloves garlic, minced

1   pound lean boneless beef, cut
     into 1-inch cubes

1   pound lean boneless pork, cut
     into 1-inch cubes

1   to 2 fresh or canned jalapeño
     peppers,* stemmed, seeded
     and minced

1   teaspoon salt

1   teaspoon dried oregano

1   teaspoon ground cumin

½   cup dry red wine

3   cups cooked pinto beans *or*
     2 cans (15 ounces each) pinto
     or kidney beans, drained

*Jalapeño peppers can sting and irritate the skin; wear
rubber gloves when handling peppers and do not touch
eyes. Wash hands after handling peppers.*

Chunky Ancho Chili with Beans

Rinse ancho chilies; remove stems, seeds and veins. Place in 2-quart pan with water. Bring to a boil; turn off heat and let stand, covered, 30 minutes or until chilies are soft. Pour chilies with liquid into blender or food processor container fitted with metal blade. Process until smooth; reserve.

Melt lard in 5-quart kettle over medium heat. Add onion and garlic; cook until onion is tender. Add beef and pork; cook, stirring frequently, until meat is lightly colored. Add jalapeño peppers, salt, oregano, cumin, wine and ancho chili purée. Bring to a boil. Cover; reduce heat and simmer 1½ to 2 hours or until meat is very tender. Stir in beans. Simmer, uncovered, 30 minutes or until chili has thickened slightly. Serve in individual bowls. *Makes 8 servings*

Variation: To make chili with chili powder, use ⅓ cup chili powder and 1½ cups water in place of ancho chili purée. Reduce salt and cumin to ½ teaspoon each.

NATIVE TO THE WESTERN HEMISPHERE, **CHILE PEPPERS** HAVE TRAVELED THE WORLD SINCE COLUMBUS' PUNGENT DISCOVERY. **HOT PEPPERS** NOW SHOW UP IN KOREA, THAILAND AND INDIA. **SCOVILLE HEAT UNITS** MEASURE THE SOURCE OF A PEPPER'S HEAT, **CAPSAICIN**. AT THE HEAD OF THE HOT LIST ARE THE **HABENERO,** THE **JAMAICAN HOT** AND, WITH PERHAPS THE MOST UNASSUMING NAME, THE **SCOTCH BONNET**.

241

HEARTY soups & stews

HEARTY soups & stews

242

1 cup chopped onion

$^1/_2$ cup chopped celery

4 teaspoons sugar

2 tablespoons chili powder

1 tablespoon dried oregano

1 teaspoon ground cumin

1 teaspoon black pepper

2 teaspoons vegetable oil

$^2/_3$ cup uncooked bulgur

$1^1/_2$ cups water

1 can (28 ounces) tomatoes, crushed or stewed

1 can (14 ounces) black beans, rinsed and drained *or* 2 cups cooked beans

1 can (14 ounces) cannellini or navy beans, rinsed and drained *or* 2 cups cooked beans

Bulgur Chili

In 3- to 4-quart saucepan, sauté onion, celery, sugar and spices in oil 5 minutes. Stir in bulgur and water. Simmer, covered, over low heat 10 minutes, stirring occasionally. Add tomatoes and beans. Simmer, covered, over low heat 15 to 20 minutes, stirring occasionally. Serve in warmed bowls.

Makes 4 servings

Favorite recipe from **The Sugar Association, Inc.**

*Food*Fact

Bulgur is a processed form of wheat produced by steaming, drying and crushing wheat kernels. It has a tender, chewy texture and comes in coarse, medium and fine grinds.

Chile Verde

½ to ¾ pound boneless lean pork

1 large onion, halved and thinly sliced

4 cloves garlic, chopped or sliced

½ cup water

1 pound fresh tomatillos

1 can (14½ ounces) ⅓-less-salt chicken broth

1 can (4 ounces) diced mild green chilies

1 teaspoon ground cumin

1½ cups cooked navy or Great Northern beans, *or* 1 can (15 ounces) Great Northern beans, rinsed and drained

½ cup lightly packed fresh cilantro, chopped

Nonfat plain yogurt (optional)

1. Trim fat from pork; discard. Cut meat into ¾- to 1-inch cubes. Place pork, onion, garlic and water in large saucepan. Cover; simmer over medium-low heat, stirring occasionally, 30 minutes (add more water if necessary). Uncover; boil over medium-high heat until liquid evaporates and meat browns.

2. Add tomatillos and broth; stir. Cover; simmer over medium heat 20 minutes or until tomatillos are tender. Tear tomatillos apart with 2 forks. Add chilies and cumin. Cover; simmer over medium-low heat 45 minutes or until meat is tender and tears apart easily (add more water or broth to keep liquid level the same). Add beans; simmer 10 minutes or until heated through. Stir in cilantro. Serve with yogurt, if desired.

Makes 4 servings

243

HEARTY *soups & stews*

HEARTY soups & stews

244

Nonstick cooking spray

1 to 1¼ pounds ground turkey (93% lean)

1 cup chopped onion

1 teaspoon bottled minced garlic

1 tablespoon chili powder

1 tablespoon ground cumin

¼ to ½ teaspoon ground red pepper

1 can (15½ ounces) chili beans in spicy sauce, undrained

1 can (14½ ounces) Mexican- or chili-style stewed or diced tomatoes, undrained

1 can (4 ounces) chopped green chilies, undrained

Santa Fe Skillet Chili

1. Spray large, deep skillet with cooking spray. Cook turkey, onion and garlic over medium-high heat, breaking meat apart with wooden spoon.

2. Sprinkle chili powder, cumin and red pepper evenly over turkey mixture; cook and stir 3 minutes or until turkey is no longer pink.

3. Stir in beans, tomatoes with juice and chilies with liquid. Reduce heat to medium; cover and simmer 10 minutes, stirring occasionally. Ladle chili into bowls.

Makes 4 servings

Serving Suggestion: Offer a variety of toppings with the skillet chili, such as chopped fresh cilantro, sour cream, shredded Cheddar or Monterey Jack cheese, and diced ripe avocado. Serve with warm corn tortillas or corn bread.

Prep and Cook Time: 19 minutes

Santa Fe Skillet Chili

- 1 pound Idaho Potatoes, peeled and cut into ½-inch cubes (about 2½ cups)
- 1 tablespoon vegetable oil
- 1 large onion, chopped (about 1 cup)
- 1 green bell pepper, diced (about 1 cup)
- 1 clove garlic, minced
- 8 ounces ground turkey
- 2 tablespoons chili powder
- 1 can (28 ounces) whole tomatoes, undrained
- 1 can (16 ounces) kidney beans, rinsed and drained
- ½ teaspoon salt
- ¼ cup chopped fresh cilantro
- ¼ cup plain nonfat yogurt *or* 2 tablespoons low-fat sour cream
- ¼ cup sliced green onions *or* chopped tomato

Idaho Potato Chili

1. Heat oil in large saucepan over medium-high heat. Add onion, pepper and garlic. Cook and stir 5 minutes or until softened.

2. Add turkey. Cook and stir 5 to 6 minutes or until no longer pink, breaking up with spoon.

3. Stir in chili powder. Cook for 1 minute. Add canned tomatoes, potatoes, beans, 1 cup water and salt. Bring to a boil. Reduce heat to low. Simmer, covered, 30 minutes, stirring occasionally.

4. Remove from heat. Stir in cilantro. Top with yogurt and green onions, if desired.   *Makes 4 to 6 servings*

Favorite recipe from **Idaho Potato Commission**

Idaho Potato Chili

2	tablespoons vegetable oil
1	pound beef round steak, cubed
2	cans (14½ ounces each) beef broth
1	can (15 ounces) dark red kidney beans, rinsed and drained
1	can (14½ ounces) tomatoes, chopped, undrained
1	medium green bell pepper, chopped
1	medium red bell pepper, chopped
1	large onion, chopped
1	large clove garlic, minced
3¼	teaspoons chili powder, divided
¼	teaspoon ground cumin
1½	cups (6 ounces) shredded JARLSBERG or JARLSBERG LITE™ Cheese, divided
¼	cup butter or margarine, softened
1	small clove garlic, minced
12	crispbreads

Chili Soup Jarlsberg

Heat oil in large, deep saucepan over medium-high heat. Add beef and cook until browned. Add beef broth; bring to a boil over high heat. Reduce heat to low. Cover and simmer 1 hour. Add kidney beans, tomatoes, red and green peppers, onion, large garlic clove, 3 teaspoons chili powder and cumin. Simmer, covered, 30 minutes. Gradually blend in ½ cup cheese. Heat just until cheese is melted.

Blend butter, small garlic clove and remaining ¼ teaspoon chili powder in small bowl. Spread on crispbreads; arrange on cookie sheet. Bake in preheated 375°F oven about 3 to 5 minutes or until butter is melted. Sprinkle with ½ cup cheese. Bake just until cheese is melted.

Ladle soup into bowls. Garnish with remaining ½ cup cheese.

Makes 6 servings

Fix-It-Fast Chili

½ pound ground beef

¾ cup chopped onion

½ teaspoon finely chopped garlic

1 can (14½ ounces) whole peeled tomatoes, undrained and chopped

1 cup water

1 package LIPTON® Rice & Sauce—Spanish

2 teaspoons chili powder

½ teaspoon ground cumin (optional)

1 cup red kidney beans, rinsed and drained

In 12-inch skillet, cook ground beef, onion and garlic over medium-high heat, stirring occasionally, 5 minutes or until browned; drain. Stir in tomatoes, water, Rice & Sauce—Spanish, chili powder and cumin and bring to a boil. Reduce heat and simmer, stirring occasionally, 10 minutes or until rice is tender. Stir in beans and heat through. Top, if desired, with shredded Cheddar cheese and crumbled corn muffins.

Makes about 4 servings

*Quick*Tip

The easiest and fastest way to peel garlic cloves is to trim off the ends and crush the cloves with the bottom of a heavy saucepan or the flat side of a large knife. The peels can then be easily removed.

249

HEARTY soups & stews

1/2   cup uncooked wheat berries

      Nonstick cooking spray

1   large onion, chopped

$\frac{1}{2}$ green bell pepper, chopped

$\frac{1}{2}$ yellow or red bell pepper, chopped

2   ribs celery, sliced

3   cloves garlic, minced

1   can ($14\frac{1}{2}$ ounces) chopped tomatoes

1   can (15 ounces) red kidney beans, rinsed and drained

1   can (15 ounces) chick-peas (garbanzo beans), rinsed and drained

$\frac{3}{4}$ cup raisins

$\frac{1}{2}$ cup water

1   tablespoon chili con carne seasoning or chili powder

1   teaspoon dried oregano leaves, crushed

1   tablespoon chopped fresh parsley

$1\frac{1}{2}$ teaspoons hot pepper sauce

Spicy Vegetable Chili

1. Place wheat berries in small saucepan and cover with 2 cups water; let soak overnight. Bring to a boil over high heat. Reduce heat to low; cover and cook 45 minutes to 1 hour or until wheat berries are tender. Drain; set aside.

2. Spray large skillet or saucepan with cooking spray; heat over medium heat. Add onion; cover and cook 5 minutes. Add bell peppers, celery and garlic; cover and cook 5 minutes, stirring occasionally.

3. Add tomatoes, kidney beans, chick-peas, raisins, water, chili seasoning, oregano and wheat berries to skillet; mix well. Bring to a boil over high heat. Reduce heat to low; simmer 25 to 30 minutes, stirring occasionally. Just before serving, stir in parsley and hot pepper sauce. Garnish, if desired.

Makes 4 servings

*Quick*Tip

Wheat berries are whole, unprocessed kernels of wheat. Look for them in health food stores and some large supermarkets.

Spicy Vegetable Chili

HEARTY soups & stews

252

1 tablespoon olive oil

1 cup chopped green bell pepper

1 cup chopped onion

1 cup sliced celery

1 clove garlic, minced

1 can (15 ounces) diced tomatoes, undrained

1 can (15 ounces) red beans, rinsed and drained

1 can (10 ounces) diced tomatoes with green chilies

1 can (8 ounces) low-sodium tomato sauce

8 (6-inch) corn tortillas

Spicy Tomato Chili with Red Beans

1. Preheat oven to 400°F.

2. Heat oil in large saucepan over medium heat until hot. Add bell pepper, onion, celery and garlic. Cook and stir 5 minutes or until onion is translucent.

3. Add remaining ingredients except tortillas. Bring to a boil; reduce heat to low. Simmer 15 minutes. Cut each tortilla into 8 wedges. Place on baking sheet; bake 8 minutes or until crisp. Crush half of tortilla wedges; place in bottom of soup bowls. Spoon chili over tortillas. Serve with remaining tortilla wedges.

Makes 4 servings

*Quick*Tip

Tortillas are the national bread of Mexico, but the popularity of Mexican cuisine has made them readily available in the U.S. Corn tortillas are made from corn flour *(masa)*, hand-shaped and baked on a round, flat griddle *(comal)*.

Spicy Tomato Chili with Red Beans

2 tablespoons vegetable oil

1 large onion, coarsely chopped

3 cloves garlic, chopped

1 medium zucchini, halved lengthwise, then thinly sliced (about 1 cup)

½ red bell pepper, cut into cubes

1 can (15 ounces) red kidney beans, rinsed and drained

1 can (15 ounces) black beans, rinsed and drained

1 can (15 ounces) garbanzo beans, rinsed and drained

1 can (15 ounces) Great Northern beans, rinsed and drained

2 cans (11 ounces each) tomatillos, drained

1 can (15 ounces) tomato sauce

½ cup barbecue sauce

1½ teaspoons ground cumin

1 to 1½ teaspoons chili powder

½ teaspoon salt

¼ to ½ teaspoon ground red pepper

Sour cream, chopped tomato, chopped onion or shredded Cheddar cheese for toppings

Flour tortillas, warmed (optional)

Chopped fresh cilantro for garnish

Four Bean Chili Stew

Heat oil in 5-quart Dutch oven over medium-high heat. Cook and stir onion and garlic in hot oil until onion is soft. Stir in zucchini and bell pepper; cook and stir 5 minutes. Add all four beans, tomatillos, tomato sauce, barbecue sauce, cumin, chili powder, salt and ground red pepper. Bring to a boil over high heat. Reduce heat to low. Cover and simmer 30 minutes. Serve with desired toppings and tortillas. Garnish with cilantro.

Makes 4 to 6 servings

QuickTip

Tomatillos are a Mexican green tomato and can be found fresh or canned in Mexican grocery stores or in the specialty food section in large supermarkets. They have a refreshing herbal flavor with a hint of lemon.

Chunky Turkey Chili

1 tablespoon butter or margarine

3/4 pound boneless turkey breast tenderloin, cut into 3/4-inch chunks

1 1/2 teaspoons bottled chopped garlic

1/2 teaspoon ground cumin

1 cup UNCLE BEN'S® ORIGINAL CONVERTED® Brand Rice

1 can (14 1/2 ounces) chili-style chunky tomatoes, undrained

1 can (15 1/2 ounces) kidney beans, drained

1 can (13 3/4 ounces) chicken broth

1. Heat butter in a large saucepan over medium heat until bubbly. Add turkey, garlic and cumin; cook and stir until turkey loses its pink color, about 3 minutes.

2. Add rice, tomatoes, kidney beans and broth. Bring to a boil over high heat. Cover; reduce heat and simmer 20 minutes, stirring occasionally.

3. Remove from heat and let stand covered 5 minutes. Stir again before serving. *Makes 4 (1 1/2-cup) servings*

Serving Suggestion: Top with chopped cilantro and shredded Monterey Jack cheese.

255

HEARTY soups & stews

2   bell peppers (red, yellow *or* green), diced into ½-inch pieces

1   medium onion, chopped (about ½ cup)

2   cloves garlic, minced

2   teaspoons oil

1   box (12 ounces) frozen BOCA® Crumbles

1   tablespoon chili powder

½   teaspoon ground cumin

1   can (4 ounces) chopped green chilies, drained

1   can (14½ ounces) diced tomatoes

1   can (15 ounces) black beans, drained

1   can (15 ounces) chili beans in sauce

1   can (15 ounces) tomato sauce

BOCA® Chili

COOK and stir peppers, onion and garlic with oil in large saucepan on medium-high heat 2 minutes. Stir in crumbles; heat 2 to 3 minutes.

ADD remaining ingredients. Bring to boil; reduce heat.

SIMMER 30 minutes, stirring occasionally. Serve with chopped tomato, green onion, reduced-fat shredded cheese, light sour cream, hot pepper sauce or other favorite toppings, if desired.   *Makes 8 (1-cup) servings*

Prep Time: 10 minutes
Cook Time: 45 minutes

*Quick*Tip

For a sweeter flavor, add 1 cup frozen kernel corn with remaining ingredients.

BOCA® Chili

1 pound lean ground beef

1 medium onion, chopped

1 tablespoon chili powder

1½ teaspoons ground cumin

2 cans (16 ounces each) diced tomatoes, undrained

1 can (15 ounces) pinto beans, drained

½ cup prepared salsa

½ cup (2 ounces) shredded Cheddar cheese

3 tablespoons sour cream

4 teaspoons sliced black olives

Quick Chunky Chili

Combine meat and onion in 3-quart saucepan; cook over high heat until meat is no longer pink, breaking meat apart with wooden spoon. Add chili powder and cumin; stir 1 minute or until fragrant. Add tomatoes with juice, beans and salsa. Bring to a boil; stir constantly. Reduce heat to low; simmer, covered, 10 minutes. Ladle into bowls. Top with cheese, sour cream and olives.

Makes 4 (1½-cup) servings

Serving Suggestion: Serve with tossed green salad and cornbread muffins.

Prep and Cook Time: 25 minutes

Quick Chunky Chili

Pork and Wild Rice Chili

1   pound boneless pork loin, cut into $^1/_2$-inch cubes

1   onion, chopped

1   teaspoon vegetable oil

2   cans (14$^1/_2$ ounces each) chicken broth

1   can (18 ounces) white kernel corn, drained

2   cans (4 ounces each) chopped green chilies, drained

$^3/_4$ cup uncooked California wild rice, rinsed

1   teaspoon ground cumin

$^1/_2$ teaspoon salt

$^1/_2$ teaspoon dried oregano leaves

1$^1/_2$ cups shredded Monterey Jack cheese (optional)

6   sprigs cilantro (optional)

Cook and stir pork and onion in oil in large saucepan over high heat until onion is soft and pork lightly browned. Add chicken broth, corn, green chilies, wild rice, cumin, salt and oregano. Cover and simmer 45 minutes or until rice is tender and grains have puffed open. Garnish with cheese and cilantro, if desired.   *Makes 6 servings*

Favorite recipe from **California Wild Rice Advisory Board**

Chicken Chili

1 pound ground chicken

1 medium onion, chopped

$^1\!/_2$ cup chopped green bell pepper

1 clove garlic, minced

2 cans (14 ounces each) diced
  tomatoes with juice

1 can (16 ounces) kidney beans,
  undrained

1 cup water

1 can (6 ounces) tomato paste

4 teaspoons chili powder

1 teaspoon salt

1 teaspoon sugar

1 teaspoon ground cumin

$^1\!/_4$ teaspoon ground red pepper

Spray nonstick Dutch oven with nonstick cooking spray; heat over medium-high heat. Add chicken, onion, bell pepper and garlic; cook, stirring, until meat is browned. Add tomatoes with juice, beans, water, tomato paste, chili powder, salt, sugar, cumin and red pepper; stir well. Reduce heat to low; simmer, uncovered, stirring occasionally, about 30 minutes.

Makes 6 servings

Favorite recipe from **Delmarva Poultry Industry, Inc.**

1   pound lean ground beef

1   can (14½ ounces) diced
      tomatoes, drained

1   cup chopped onion

1   clove garlic, minced

½   teaspoon salt

½   teaspoon ground cumin

½   teaspoon dried oregano leaves

¼   teaspoon black pepper

¼   teaspoon red pepper flakes

1   tablespoon chili powder

2   cups cooked macaroni

Hearty Chili Mac

Crumble ground beef into slow cooker. Add remaining ingredients, except macaroni, to slow cooker. Cover and cook on LOW 4 hours. Stir in cooked macaroni. Cover and cook on LOW 1 hour.   *Makes 4 servings*

Quick Tip

Two great advantages of the slow cooker are that it doesn't heat up the kitchen, and the long cooking time provides the cook hours of freedom.

Hearty Chili Mac

1¼ cups dried pinto beans

1 pound ground beef or turkey

1 onion, chopped

3 tablespoons Hearty Chili Seasoning Mix (recipe follows)

1 can (28 ounces) diced tomatoes, undrained

1 can (about 14 ounces) beef broth

Hearty Chili

1. Place beans and 8 cups cold water in large saucepan. Bring to a boil over high heat. Boil 1 minute. Remove saucepan from heat. Cover; let stand 1 hour.

2. Drain beans; rinse under cold running water. Return beans to saucepan. Add 8 cups cold water. Bring to a boil over high heat. Reduce heat to medium-low. Simmer 1 hour 15 minutes or until beans are just tender, stirring occasionally. Remove saucepan from heat and drain beans; set aside. Combine beef and onion in large saucepan. Cook over medium-high heat 6 minutes or until beef is no longer pink, stirring to crumble beef. Spoon off and discard any drippings.

3. Add seasoning mix to saucepan. Cook 1 minute, stirring frequently. Add beans, tomatoes with juice and beef broth; bring to a boil over high heat. Reduce heat to medium-low. Cover; simmer 30 minutes, stirring occasionally. Store in airtight container in refrigerator up to 3 days or freeze up to 1 month.

Makes about 8 cups

Hearty Chili Seasoning Mix

½ cup chili powder

¼ cup ground cumin

2 tablespoons *each* garlic salt and dried oregano

2 teaspoons ground coriander

½ teaspoon ground red pepper

Combine all ingredients in small bowl. Store in airtight container with spices up to 3 months.   *Makes about 1 cup*

Reci-

ipe: HEARTY CHILI
SEASONING MIX

1 CUP CHILI POWDER
1 CUP GROUND CUMIN
2 TABLESPOONS DRIED OREGANO
2 TABLESPOONS GARLIC SALT
2 TEASPOONS GROUND CORIANDER
1/2 TEASPOON GROUND RED
       PEPPER

Hearty Chili

1 pound ground beef

1 package (about 1¾ ounces) chili seasoning mix

1 can (16 ounces) whole kernel corn, drained

1 can (14½ ounces) tomatoes, undrained and cut up

½ cup water

¾ cup biscuit baking mix

⅔ cup cornmeal

⅔ cup milk

1⅓ cups *French's®* Taste Toppers™ French Fried Onions, divided

½ cup (2 ounces) shredded Monterey Jack cheese

Texas Chili & Biscuits

Preheat oven to 400°F. In medium skillet, brown beef; drain. Stir in chili seasoning, corn, tomatoes with juice and water; bring to a boil. Reduce heat; simmer, uncovered, 10 minutes.

Meanwhile, in medium bowl, combine baking mix, cornmeal, milk and ⅔ cup **Taste Toppers**; beat vigorously 30 seconds. Pour beef mixture into 2-quart casserole. Spoon biscuit dough in mounds around edge of casserole.

Bake, uncovered, at 400°F for 15 minutes or until biscuits are light brown. Top biscuits with cheese and remaining ⅔ cup **Taste Toppers**; bake, uncovered, 1 to 3 minutes or until **Taste Toppers** are golden brown.   *Makes 4 to 6 servings*

QuickTip

The addition of beans to chili is a hotly-debated topic among chili aficionados. While many consider beans a necessity, Texans never add beans to their "bowls of red." The beanless way is so strongly upheld in Texas that on the streets of San Antonio, bean-loving chili eaters are a scarce breed.

Vegetable Chili

2   cans (15 ounces each) chunky chili tomato sauce

1   bag (16 ounces) BIRDS EYE® frozen Farm Fresh Mixtures Broccoli, Corn and Red Peppers

1   can (15½ ounces) red kidney beans

1   can (4½ ounces) chopped green chilies

½   cup shredded Cheddar cheese

• Combine tomato sauce, vegetables, beans and chilies in large saucepan; bring to boil.

• Cook, uncovered, over medium heat 5 minutes.

• Sprinkle individual servings with cheese.

Makes 4 to 6 servings

Prep Time: 5 minutes
Cook Time: 10 minutes

267

HEARTY *soups & stews*

1½   pounds lean ground beef

1   medium onion, chopped

2   tablespoons chili powder

1   can (19 ounces) red kidney beans, rinsed and drained

1   jar (26 to 28 ounces) RAGÚ® Old World Style® Pasta Sauce

1   cup shredded Cheddar cheese (about 4 ounces)

Rapid Ragú® Chili

1. In 12-inch skillet, brown ground beef with onion and chili powder over medium-high heat, stirring occasionally. Stir in beans and Ragú Pasta Sauce.

2. Bring to a boil over high heat. Reduce heat to low and simmer covered, stirring occasionally, 20 minutes. Top with cheese. Serve, if desired, over hot cooked rice.

Makes 6 servings

Prep Time: 10 minutes
Cook Time: 25 minutes

*Quick*Tip

When choosing lean ground beef, look for "loin" or "round" in the name, such as ground sirloin or ground round. These have only about 11 percent fat, whereas ground chuck contains about 15 to 20 percent and hamburger contains up to 30 percent.

Rapid Ragú® Chili

HEARTY soups & stews

270

1   package (6.8 ounces) RICE-A-RONI® Spanish Rice

2¾   cups water

2   cups chopped cooked chicken or turkey

1   can (15 or 16 ounces) kidney beans or pinto beans, rinsed and drained

1   can (14½ or 16 ounces) tomatoes or stewed tomatoes, undrained

1   medium green bell pepper, cut into ½-inch pieces

1½   teaspoons chili powder

1   teaspoon ground cumin

½   cup (2 ounces) shredded Cheddar or Monterey Jack cheese (optional)

     Sour cream (optional)

     Chopped cilantro (optional)

Tex-Mex Chicken & Rice Chili

1. In 3-quart saucepan, combine rice-vermicelli mix, Special Seasonings, water, chicken, beans, tomatoes with juice, green pepper, chili powder and cumin. Bring to a boil over high heat.

2. Reduce heat to low; simmer, uncovered, about 20 minutes or until rice is tender, stirring occasionally.

3. Top with cheese, sour cream and cilantro, if desired.

Makes 4 servings

Tex-Mex Chicken & Rice Chili

Good things *come to those who wait, not to mention those who* use their **slow cookers.** *Dust yours off and let it do all the work. There's nothing better than coming home to hot, thick* **ready-to-eat** *soups and stews.*

1   cup dried lentils, rinsed and drained

1   package (16 ounces) frozen green beans

2   cups cauliflower florets

1   cup chopped onion

1   cup baby carrots, cut in half crosswise

3   cups fat-free reduced-sodium chicken broth

2   teaspoons ground cumin

3/4   teaspoon ground ginger

1   can (15 ounces) chunky tomato sauce with garlic and herbs

1/2   cup dry-roasted peanuts

Hearty Lentil Stew

1. Place lentils in slow cooker. Top with green beans, cauliflower, onion and carrots. Combine broth, cumin and ginger in large bowl; mix well. Pour mixture over vegetables. Cover and cook on LOW 9 to 11 hours.

2. Stir in tomato sauce. Cover and cook on LOW 10 minutes. Ladle stew into bowls. Sprinkle peanuts evenly over each serving.   *Makes 6 servings*

Hearty Lentil Stew

274

1   can (14½ ounces) diced tomatoes, undrained

1   can (10½ ounces) condensed beef broth, undiluted

1   package (8 ounces) sliced mushrooms

1   medium zucchini, thinly sliced

1   medium green bell pepper, chopped

1   medium yellow onion, chopped

⅓   cup dry red wine or beef broth

1½   tablespoons dried basil leaves

2½   teaspoons sugar

1   tablespoon extra virgin olive oil

½   teaspoon salt

1   cup (4 ounces) shredded Mozzarella cheese (optional)

Easy Italian Vegetable Soup

1. Combine tomatoes, broth, mushrooms, zucchini, bell pepper, onion, wine, basil and sugar in slow cooker. Cook on LOW 8 hours or on HIGH 4 hours.

2. Stir oil and salt into soup. Garnish with cheese, if desired.

Makes 5 to 6 servings

Quick Tip

Choose zucchini that are heavy for their size, firm and well shaped. They should have a bright color and be free of cuts and any soft spots. Small zucchini are more tender because they were harvested when they were young.

Easy Italian Vegetable Soup

HEARTY soups & stews

Caribbean Shrimp with Rice

1 package (12 ounces) frozen shrimp, thawed

½ cup chicken broth

1 clove garlic, minced

1 teaspoon chili powder

½ teaspoon salt

½ teaspoon dried oregano leaves

1 cup frozen peas

½ cup diced tomatoes

2 cups cooked rice

Slow Cooker Directions

Combine shrimp, broth, garlic, chili powder, salt and oregano in slow cooker. Cover and cook on LOW 2 hours. Add peas and tomatoes. Cover and cook on LOW 5 minutes. Stir in rice. Cover and cook on LOW an additional 5 minutes.

Makes 4 servings

Caribbean Shrimp with Rice

278

4 pounds beef short ribs, trimmed

2 pounds small red potatoes, scrubbed and scored

8 carrots, peeled and cut into chunks

2 onions, cut into thick wedges

1 bottle (12 ounces) beer or non-alcoholic malt beverage

8 tablespoons *French's*® Hearty Deli Brown Mustard, divided

3 tablespoons *French's*® Worcestershire Sauce, divided

2 tablespoons cornstarch

Deviled Beef Short Rib Stew

Slow Cooker Directions

1. Broil ribs 6 inches from heat on rack in broiler pan 10 minutes or until well-browned, turning once. Place potatoes and vegetables in bottom of slow cooker. Place ribs on top of vegetables.

2. Combine beer, *6 tablespoons* mustard and *2 tablespoons* Worcestershire in medium bowl. Pour into slow cooker. Cover and cook on HIGH 5 hours* or until meat is tender.

3. Transfer meat and vegetables to platter; keep warm. Strain fat from broth; pour into saucepan. Combine cornstarch with *2 tablespoons cold water* in small bowl. Stir into broth with remaining *2 tablespoons* mustard and *1 tablespoon* Worcestershire. Heat to boiling. Reduce heat to medium-low. Cook 1 to 2 minutes or until thickened, stirring often. Pass gravy with meat and vegetables. Serve meat with additional mustard.   *Makes 6 servings (with 3 cups gravy)*

Or cook 10 hours on LOW-heat setting.

Tip: Prepare ingredients the night before for quick assembly in the morning. Keep refrigerated until ready to use.

Prep Time: 20 minutes
Cook Time: 5 minutes

Deviled Beef Short Rib Stew

2   cans (14½ ounces each) reduced-sodium beef broth

1   can (14½ ounces) diced tomatoes, undrained

1   cup diced potato

1   cup coarsely chopped green cabbage

1   cup coarsely chopped carrots

1   cup sliced zucchini

¾   cup chopped onion

¾   cup sliced fresh green beans

¾   cup coarsely chopped celery

¾   cup water

2   tablespoons olive oil

1   clove garlic, minced

½   teaspoon dried basil leaves

¼   teaspoon dried rosemary

1   bay leaf

1   can (15½ ounces) cannellini beans, rinsed and drained

Grated Parmesan cheese (optional)

Minestrone alla Milanese

Slow Cooker Directions

Combine all ingredients except cannellini beans and cheese in slow cooker; mix well. Cover and cook on LOW 5 to 6 hours. Add cannellini beans. Cover and cook on LOW 1 hour or until vegetables are crisp-tender. Remove and discard bay leaf. Garnish with cheese, if desired.

Makes 8 to 10 servings

QuickTip

When using a slow cooker, dense vegetables such as potatoes and carrots should be cut into pieces no larger than 1 inch thick so they will cook through.

Minestrone alla Milanese

Chicken and Chili Pepper Stew

1 pound boneless skinless chicken thighs, cut into ½-inch pieces

1 pound small potatoes, cut lengthwise into halves and then cut crosswise into slices

1 cup chopped onion

2 poblano chili peppers, seeded and cut into ½-inch pieces

1 jalapeño pepper, seeded and finely chopped

3 cloves garlic, minced

3 cups fat-free reduced-sodium chicken broth

1 can (14½ ounces) no-salt-added diced tomatoes

2 tablespoons chili powder

1 teaspoon dried oregano leaves

1. Place chicken, potatoes, onion, poblano peppers, jalapeño pepper and garlic in slow cooker.

2. Stir together broth, tomatoes, chili powder and oregano in large bowl. Pour broth mixture over chicken mixture in slow cooker. Stir. Cover and cook on LOW 8 to 9 hours.

Makes 6 servings

*Food*Fact

Poblano peppers are very dark green, large, triangular-shaped chilies with pointed ends. Poblanos are usually 3½ to 5 inches long and their flavor ranges from mild to quite hot. For a milder flavor, Anaheims can be substituted.

Hungarian Lamb Goulash

1 package (16 ounces) frozen cut green beans

1 cup chopped onion

1¼ pounds lean lamb stew meat, cut into 1-inch pieces

1 can (15 ounces) chunky tomato sauce

1¾ cups reduced-sodium chicken broth

1 can (6 ounces) tomato paste

4 teaspoons paprika

3 cups hot cooked noodles

Slow Cooker Directions

Place green beans and onion in slow cooker. Top with lamb. Combine remaining ingredients, except noodles in large bowl; mix well. Pour over lamb mixture. Cover and cook on LOW 6 to 8 hours. Stir. Serve over noodles. *Makes 6 servings*

283

HEARTY soups & stews

6   cups chicken broth

¾   pound potatoes, peeled and diced

1   can (16 ounces) black beans, drained

½   pound ham, diced

½   onion, diced

1   can (4 ounces) chopped jalapeño peppers*

2   cloves garlic, minced

2   teaspoons dried oregano leaves

1½   teaspoons dried thyme leaves

1   teaspoon ground cumin

   Sour cream, chopped bell peppers and chopped tomatoes for garnish

Jalapeño peppers can sting and irritate the skin; wear rubber gloves when handling peppers and do not touch eyes. Wash hands after handling.

Fiesta Black Bean Soup

Slow Cooker Directions

Combine all ingredients, except garnish, in slow cooker. Cover and cook on LOW 8 to 10 hours or on HIGH 4 to 5 hours. Garnish, if desired.   *Makes 6 to 8 servings*

*Food*Fact

The goodness of beans is indeed a cause for celebration! Beans are rich in protein, calcium, phosphorus and iron, making any bean-based meal a festival of nutrients.

Fiesta Black Bean Soup

286

2 medium all-purpose potatoes,
   thinly sliced (about 1 pound)

2 medium carrots, sliced

4 bone-in chicken pieces (about
   2 pounds)

1 envelope LIPTON® RECIPE
   SECRETS® Savory Herb with
   Garlic Soup Mix

⅓ cup water

1 tablespoon olive or vegetable oil

Herbed Chicken & Vegetables

1. Preheat oven to 425°F. In broiler pan, without the rack, place potatoes and carrots; arrange chicken on top. Pour soup mix blended with water and oil over chicken and vegetables.

2. Bake uncovered 40 minutes or until chicken is no longer pink and vegetables are tender.   *Makes 4 servings*

Slow Cooker Method: Place all ingredients in slow cooker, arranging chicken on top; cover. Cook on HIGH 4 hours or LOW 6 to 8 hours.

Prep Time: 10 minutes
Cook Time: 40 minutes

Herbed Chicken & Vegetables

Hearty Cassoulet

1 tablespoon olive oil

1 large onion, finely chopped

4 boneless skinless chicken thighs (about 1 pound), chopped

1/4 pound smoked turkey sausage, finely chopped

3 cloves garlic, minced

1 teaspoon dried thyme leaves

1/2 teaspoon black pepper

4 tablespoons tomato paste

2 tablespoons water

3 cans (about 15 ounces each) Great Northern beans, rinsed and drained

1/2 cup dry bread crumbs

3 tablespoons minced fresh parsley

Slow Cooker Directions

Heat oil in large skillet over medium heat until hot. Add onion. Cook and stir 5 minutes or until onion is tender. Stir in chicken, sausage, garlic, thyme and pepper. Cook 5 minutes or until chicken and sausage are browned.

Remove skillet from heat; stir in tomato paste and water until blended. Place beans and chicken mixture in slow cooker. Cover and cook on LOW 4 to 4 1/2 hours. Just before serving, combine bread crumbs and parsley in small bowl. Sprinkle top of cassoulet. *Makes 6 servings*

Hearty Cassoulet

Pork Stew

2 tablespoons vegetable oil, divided

3 pounds fresh lean boneless pork butt, cut into 1½-inch cubes

2 medium white onions, thinly sliced

3 cloves garlic, minced

1 teaspoon salt

1 teaspoon ground cumin

¾ teaspoon dried oregano leaves

1 can (8 ounces) tomatillos, drained and chopped *or* 1 cup husked and chopped fresh tomatillos

1 can (4 ounces) chopped green chilies, drained

½ cup reduced-sodium chicken broth

1 large tomato, peeled and coarsely chopped

¼ cup fresh cilantro, chopped *or* ½ teaspoon ground coriander

2 teaspoons lime juice

4 cups hot cooked white rice

½ cup toasted slivered almonds (optional)

Slow Cooker Directions

Heat 1 tablespoon oil in large skillet over medium heat. Add pork; cook 10 minutes or until browned on all sides. Remove and set aside. Heat remaining 1 tablespoon oil in skillet. Add onions, garlic, salt, cumin and oregano; cook and stir 2 minutes or until soft.

Combine pork, onion mixture and remaining ingredients except rice and almonds in slow cooker; mix well. Cover and cook on LOW 5 hours or until pork is tender and barely pink in center. Serve over rice and sprinkle with almonds, if desired.

Makes 10 servings

Double Thick Baked Potato-Cheese Soup

2 pounds baking potatoes, peeled and cut into ½-inch cubes

2 cans (10½-ounces each) cream of mushroom soup

1½ cups finely chopped green onions, divided

¼ teaspoon garlic powder

⅛ teaspoon ground red pepper

1½ cups (6 ounces) shredded sharp Cheddar cheese

1 cup (8 ounces) sour cream

1 cup milk

Black pepper

1. Combine potatoes, soup, 1 cup green onions, garlic powder and red pepper in slow cooker. Cover and cook on HIGH 4 hours or on LOW 8 hours.

2. Add cheese, sour cream and milk; stir until cheese has completely melted. Cover and cook on HIGH an additional 10 minutes. Season to taste with black pepper. Garnish with remaining green onions. *Makes 7 servings*

291

HEARTY *soups & stews*

Mediterranean Meatball Ratatouille

2 tablespoons olive oil, divided

1 pound mild Italian sausage, casings removed

1 package (8 ounces) sliced mushrooms, divided

1 small eggplant, diced

1 zucchini, diced

½ cup chopped onion

1 clove garlic, minced

1 teaspoon dried oregano leaves, divided

1 teaspoon salt, divided

½ teaspoon black pepper, divided

1 tablespoon tomato paste

2 tomatoes, diced

2 tablespoons chopped fresh basil

1 teaspoon fresh lemon juice

1. Pour 1 tablespoon olive oil into 5-quart slow cooker. Shape sausage into 1-inch meatballs. Place half the meatballs in slow cooker. Add half the mushrooms, eggplant and zucchini. Add onion, garlic, ½ teaspoon oregano, ½ teaspoon salt and ¼ teaspoon pepper.

2. Add remaining meatballs, mushrooms, eggplant and zucchini. Add remaining oregano, salt and pepper. Top with remaining olive oil. Cover and cook on LOW 6 to 7 hours.

3. Stir in tomato paste and diced tomatoes. Cover and cook on LOW 15 minutes. Stir in basil and lemon; serve.

Makes 6 (1⅔-cups) servings

Mediterranean Meatball Ratatouille

HEARTY soups & stews

294

4 cups chicken broth

3 potatoes, peeled and diced

1½ cups chopped cabbage

1 leek, diced

1 onion, chopped

2 carrots, diced

¼ cup chopped fresh parsley

2 teaspoons salt

2 teaspoons black pepper

½ teaspoon caraway seeds

1 bay leaf

½ cup sour cream

1 pound bacon, cooked and crumbled

Potato and Leek Soup

Slow Cooker Directions

Combine chicken broth, potatoes, cabbage, leek, onion, carrots and parsley in large bowl; pour mixture into slow cooker. Stir in salt, pepper, caraway seeds and bay leaf. Cover and cook on LOW 8 to 10 hours or on HIGH 4 to 5 hours. Remove and discard bay leaf. Combine some hot liquid from slow cooker with sour cream in small bowl. Add mixture to slow cooker; stir. Stir in bacon. *Makes 6 to 8 servings*

*Quick*Tip

Leeks are notorious for collecting soil and grit between the leaf layers. Make a deep cut into each leek lengthwise to within an inch of the root end. (If the leek is cut into halves it will fall apart.) Rinse leeks thoroughly under cold running water to remove embedded soil. To remove stubborn dirt, soak them in a bowl of water for 15 minutes, changing the water until it is clear and the leeks are free of dirt.

Potato and Leek Soup

Bean Ragoût with Cilantro-Cornmeal Dumplings

2   cans (14$\frac{1}{2}$ ounces each) tomatoes, chopped and undrained

1$\frac{1}{2}$ cups chopped red bell pepper

1   large onion, chopped

1   can (15$\frac{1}{2}$ ounces) pinto or kidney beans, rinsed and drained

1   can (15$\frac{1}{2}$ ounces) black beans, rinsed and drained

2   small zucchini, sliced

$\frac{1}{2}$ cup chopped green bell pepper

$\frac{1}{2}$ cup chopped celery

1   poblano chili pepper, seeded and chopped

2   cloves garlic, minced

3   tablespoons chili powder

2   teaspoons ground cumin

1   teaspoon dried oregano leaves

$\frac{1}{2}$ teaspoon salt, divided

$\frac{1}{8}$ teaspoon black pepper

$\frac{1}{4}$ cup all-purpose flour

$\frac{1}{4}$ cup yellow cornmeal

$\frac{1}{2}$ teaspoon baking powder

1   tablespoon vegetable shortening

2   tablespoons shredded Cheddar cheese

2   teaspoons minced fresh cilantro

$\frac{1}{4}$ cup milk

Slow Cooker Directions

Combine tomatoes with juice, red bell pepper, onion, beans, zucchini, green bell pepper, celery, poblano pepper, garlic, chili powder, cumin, oregano, $\frac{1}{4}$ teaspoon salt and black pepper in slow cooker; mix well. Cover and cook on LOW 7 to 8 hours.

Prepare dumplings 1 hour before serving. Mix flour, cornmeal, baking powder and remaining $\frac{1}{4}$ teaspoon salt in medium bowl. Cut in shortening with pastry blender or two knives until mixture resembles coarse crumbs. Stir in cheese and cilantro. Pour milk into flour mixture. Blend just until dry ingredients are moistened. Turn slow cooker to HIGH. Drop dumplings by level tablespoonfuls (larger dumplings will not cook properly) on top of ragoût. Cover and cook 1 hour or until toothpick inserted in dumpling comes out clean.

Makes 6 servings

Bean Ragoût with Cilantro-Cornmeal Dumplings

HEARTY soups & stews

298

1 package (8 ounces) sliced mushrooms

1 package (8 ounces) baby carrots

1 medium green bell pepper, cut into thin strips

1 boneless chuck roast (2½ pounds)

1 can (10½ ounces) golden mushroom soup

¼ cup dry red wine or beef broth

1 tablespoon Worcestershire sauce

1 package (1 ounce) dried onion soup mix

¼ teaspoon black pepper

2 tablespoons water

3 tablespoons cornstarch

4 cups hot cooked noodles

Chopped fresh parsley (optional)

Beef and Vegetables in Rich Burgundy Sauce

1. Place mushrooms, carrots and bell pepper in slow cooker. Place roast on top of vegetables. Combine soup, wine, Worcestershire sauce, soup mix and black pepper in medium bowl; mix well. Pour soup mixture over roast. Cover and cook on LOW 8 to 10 hours.

2. Blend water into cornstarch in cup until smooth; set aside. Transfer roast to cutting board; cover with foil. Let stand 10 to 15 minutes before slicing.

3. Turn slow cooker to HIGH. Stir cornstarch mixture into vegetable mixture; cover and cook 10 minutes or until thickened. Serve over cooked noodles. Garnish with parsley, if desired.

Makes 6 to 8 servings

Beef and Vegetables in Rich Burgundy Sauce

300

3 cans (15 ounces each) black beans, drained and rinsed

1½ cups chopped onion

1½ cups fat-free reduced-sodium chicken broth

1 cup sliced celery

1 cup chopped red bell pepper

4 cloves garlic, minced

1½ teaspoons dried oregano

¾ teaspoon ground coriander

½ teaspoon ground cumin

¼ teaspoon ground red pepper

6 ounces cooked turkey sausage, thinly sliced

Black Bean and Sausage Stew

1. Combine all ingredients in slow cooker, except sausage. Cover and cook on LOW 6 to 8 hours.

2. Remove about 1½ cups bean mixture from slow cooker to blender or food processor; purée bean mixture. Return to slow cooker. Stir in sliced sausage. Cover and cook on LOW an additional 10 to 15 minutes.   *Makes 6 servings*

*Food*Fact

Most U.S. turkeys raised today are from the White Holland variety,

which has been bred to produce a maximum of white meat (a

U.S. favorite).

Chunky Vegetable Chili

1 medium onion, chopped

2 ribs celery, diced

1 carrot, diced

3 cloves garlic, minced

2 cans (about 15 ounces each)
   Great Northern beans, rinsed
   and drained

1 cup water

1 cup frozen corn

1 can (6 ounces) tomato paste

1 can (4 ounces) diced mild green
   chilies, undrained

1 tablespoon chili powder

2 teaspoons dried oregano leaves

1 teaspoon salt

Slow Cooker Directions

Combine all ingredients in slow cooker. Cover and cook on
LOW 5½ to 6 hours or until vegetables are tender.

Makes 6 servings

301

HEARTY *soups & stews*

8 ounces kielbasa sausage, cut in
   $1/4$-inch slices

1 can ($14^1/2$ ounces) diced
   tomatoes, undrained

1 medium onion, diced

1 medium green bell pepper, diced

2 celery stalks, thinly sliced

1 tablespoon chicken bouillon
   granules

1 tablespoon steak sauce

3 bay leaves *or* 1 teaspoon dried
   thyme leaves

1 teaspoon sugar

$1/4$ to $1/2$ teaspoon hot pepper sauce

1 cup uncooked instant rice

$1/2$ cup chopped parsley (optional)

Cajun Sausage and Rice

1. Combine sausage, tomatoes, onion, pepper, celery, bouillon, steak sauce, bay leaves, sugar and hot pepper sauce in slow cooker. Cover and cook on LOW 8 hours or on HIGH 4 hours.

2. Remove bay leaves; stir in rice and ½ cup water. Cook an additional 25 minutes. Stir in parsley, if desired.

Makes 5 servings

*Food*Fact

Cajuns are the descendants of French Acadians who were forced from their Nova Scotian homeland by the British in 1785 and transplanted to Louisiana. It comes as no surprise that Cajun cooking is a blend of French and Southern cuisines, featuring robust flavors, the liberal use of spices and the beloved threesome of chopped green peppers, onions and celery.

Pork and Mushroom Ragoût

Nonstick cooking spray

1   boneless pork loin roast
    (1¼-pounds)

1¼ cups canned crushed tomatoes,
    divided

2   tablespoons cornstarch

2   teaspoons dried savory leaves

3   sun-dried tomatoes, patted dry
    and chopped

1   package (8 ounces) sliced
    mushrooms

1   large onion, sliced

1   teaspoon black pepper

3   cups hot cooked noodles

1. Spray large nonstick skillet with cooking spray; heat over medium heat until hot. Brown roast on all sides; set aside.

2. Combine ½ cup crushed tomatoes, cornstarch, savory and sun-dried tomatoes in large bowl. Pour mixture into slow cooker. Layer mushrooms, onion and roast over tomato mixture. Pour remaining tomatoes over roast; sprinkle with pepper. Cover and cook on LOW 4 to 6 hours or until internal temperature reaches 165°F when tested with meat thermometer inserted into thickest part of roast.

3. Remove roast from slow cooker. Transfer roast to cutting board; cover with foil. Let stand 10 to 15 minutes before slicing. Internal temperature will continue to rise 5° to 10°F during stand time. Serve over hot cooked noodles.

Makes 6 servings

303

HEARTY *soups & stews*

OZOLE BISQUE

TOU CIOPPINO

2 cans (about 14 ounces each) beef broth, divided

1/3 cup all-purpose flour

1 1/2 pounds pork tenderloin, trimmed and diced

4 red potatoes, unpeeled and cut into cubes

2 cups frozen cut green beans

1 onion, chopped

2 cloves garlic, minced

1 teaspoon salt

1 teaspoon dried thyme leaves

1/2 teaspoon black pepper

304

Stew Provençal

Slow Cooker Directions

Combine 3/4 cup beef broth and flour in small bowl. Set aside.

Add remaining broth, pork, potatoes, beans, onion, garlic, salt, thyme and pepper to slow cooker; stir. Cover and cook on LOW 8 to 10 hours or on HIGH 4 to 5 hours. If cooking on LOW, turn to HIGH last 30 minutes. Stir in flour mixture. Cover and cook 30 minutes to thicken.   *Makes 8 servings*

Stew Provençal

Savory Pea Soup with Sausage

8 ounces smoked sausage, cut lengthwise into halves, then cut into ¹/₂-inch pieces

2 cans (14¹/₂ ounces each) reduced-sodium chicken broth

1 package (16 ounces) dried split peas, sorted and rinsed

3 medium carrots, sliced

2 ribs celery, sliced

1 medium onion, chopped

³/₄ teaspoon dried marjoram leaves

1 bay leaf

Slow Cooker Directions

Heat small skillet over medium heat. Add sausage; cook 5 to 8 minutes or until browned. Drain well. Combine sausage and remaining ingredients in slow cooker. Cover and cook on LOW 4 to 5 hours or until peas are tender. Turn off heat. Remove and discard bay leaf. Cover and let stand 15 minutes to thicken.   *Makes 6 servings*

Savory Pea Soup with Sausage

Lentil Stew over Couscous

1 large onion, chopped

1 green bell pepper, chopped

4 ribs celery, chopped

1 medium carrot, cut lengthwise into halves, then cut into 1-inch pieces

2 cloves garlic, chopped

3 cups lentils (1 pound), rinsed

1 can (14½ ounces) diced tomatoes, undrained

1 can (14½ ounces) reduced-sodium chicken broth

3 cups water

¼ teaspoon black pepper

1 teaspoon dried marjoram leaves

1 tablespoon cider vinegar

1 tablespoon olive oil

4½ to 5 cups hot cooked couscous

Carrot curls (optional)

Celery leaves (optional)

Slow Cooker Directions

Combine onion, green bell pepper, celery, carrot, garlic, lentils, tomatoes, broth, water, black pepper and marjoram in slow cooker. Stir; cover and cook on LOW 8 to 9 hours.

Stir in vinegar and olive oil. Serve over couscous. Garnish with carrot curls and celery leaves, if desired.

Makes 12 servings

Tip: Lentil stew keeps well in the refrigerator for up to one week. Stew can also be frozen in airtight container in freezer up to three months.

Turkey-Tomato Soup

2 medium turkey thighs, boned, skinned and cut into 1-inch pieces

2 small white or red potatoes, cubed

1¾ cups fat-free reduced-sodium chicken broth

1½ cups frozen corn

1 cup chopped onion

1 cup water

1 can (8 ounces) no-salt-added tomato sauce

¼ cup tomato paste

2 tablespoons Dijon mustard

1 teaspoon hot pepper sauce

½ teaspoon sugar

½ teaspoon garlic powder

¼ cup finely chopped parsley

Combine all ingredients, except parsley, in slow cooker. Cover and cook on LOW 9 to 10 hours. Stir in parsley; serve.

Makes 6 servings

309

HEARTY *soups & stews*

1 boneless, beef sirloin tip roast (1¼ pounds)

3 cups baby carrots

1½ cups fresh or frozen pearl onions

¼ cup raisins

½ cup water

½ cup red wine vinegar

1 tablespoon honey

½ teaspoon salt

½ teaspoon dry mustard

½ teaspoon garlic-pepper seasoning

¼ teaspoon ground cloves

¼ cup crushed crisp gingersnap cookies (5 cookies)

Sauerbraten

Slow Cooker Directions

1. Heat large nonstick skillet over medium heat until hot. Brown roast on all sides; set aside.

2. Place roast, carrots, onions and raisins in slow cooker. Combine water, vinegar, honey, salt, mustard, garlic-pepper seasoning and cloves in large bowl; mix well. Pour mixture over meat and vegetables.

3. Cover and cook on LOW 4 to 6 hours or until internal temperature reaches 145°F when tested with meat thermometer inserted into thickest part of roast. Transfer roast to cutting board; cover with foil. Let stand 10 to 15 minutes before slicing. Internal temperature will continue to rise 5° to 10°F during stand time.

4. Remove vegetables with slotted spoon to bowl; cover to keep warm. Stir crushed cookies into sauce mixture in slow cooker. Cover and cook on HIGH 10 to 15 minutes or until sauce thickens. Serve meat and vegetables with sauce.

Makes 5 servings

Sauerbraten

2 pounds beef stew meat, cut into
    1-inch pieces

1 tablespoon vegetable oil

1 jar (4 ounces) sliced
    mushrooms, drained

1/4 cup minced onion

3 cloves garlic, minced

1 teaspoon salt

1 teaspoon black pepper

1/8 teaspoon dried thyme

1 bay leaf

1 can (13 3/4 ounces) beef broth

1/3 cup cooking sherry

1 carton (8 ounces) sour cream

1/2 cup all-purpose flour

1/4 cup water

4 cups hot cooked noodles

Creamy Beef and Noodles

Brown beef in hot oil in large skillet. Drain off fat.

Combine beef, mushrooms, onion, garlic, salt, pepper, thyme and bay leaf in slow cooker. Pour in beef broth and sherry. Cover and cook on LOW 8 to 10 hours. Discard bay leaf.

Increase heat to HIGH. Combine sour cream, flour and water in small bowl. Stir about 1 cup of hot liquid into sour cream mixture. Return to slow cooker; stir. Cover and cook on HIGH 30 minutes or until thickened and bubbly. Serve over noodles.

Makes 6 to 8 servings

Golden Harvest Stew

1 pound pork cutlets, cut into
1-inch pieces

2 tablespoons all-purpose flour,
divided

1 tablespoon vegetable oil

2 medium Yukon gold potatoes,
unpeeled and cut into 1-inch
cubes

1 large sweet potato, peeled and
cut into 1-inch cubes

1 cup chopped carrots

1 ear corn, broken into 4 pieces *or*
$^1/_2$ cup canned corn

$^1/_2$ cup chicken broth

1 jalapeño pepper, seeded and
finely chopped

1 clove garlic, minced

1 teaspoon salt

$^1/_4$ teaspoon black pepper

$^1/_4$ teaspoon dried thyme leaves

1. Coat pork pieces with 1 tablespoon flour; set aside. Heat oil in large nonstick skillet over medium-high heat until hot. Brown pork 2 to 3 minutes per side; transfer to 5-quart slow cooker.

2. Add remaining ingredients to slow cooker. Cover and cook on LOW 5 to 6 hours.

3. Combine remaining 1 tablespoon flour and $^1/_4$ cup broth from stew in small bowl; stir until smooth. Pour flour mixture into stew; stir. Cover and cook on HIGH 10 minutes.

Makes 4 (2$^1/_2$-cup) servings

Classic French Onion Soup

1/4 cup butter

3 large yellow onions, sliced

1 cup dry white wine

3 cans (about 14 ounces each) beef or chicken broth

1 teaspoon Worcestershire sauce

1/2 teaspoon salt

1/2 teaspoon dried thyme

1 loaf French bread, sliced and toasted

4 ounces shredded Swiss cheese

Fresh thyme for garnish

Slow Cooker Directions

Melt butter in large skillet over high heat. Add onions, cook and stir 15 minutes or until onions are soft and lightly browned. Stir in wine.

Combine onion mixture, beef broth, Worcestershire, salt and thyme in slow cooker. Cover and cook on LOW 4 to 4½ hours. Ladle soup into 4 individual bowls; top with bread slice and cheese. Garnish with fresh thyme, if desired.

Makes 4 servings

Classic French Onion Soup

1 cup chicken broth

1 can (14½ ounces) diced
    tomatoes, undrained

¼ cup all-purpose flour

2 tablespoons olive oil

¾ pound Polish sausage, cut into
    ½-inch pieces

1 medium onion, diced

1 green bell pepper, diced

2 ribs celery, chopped

1 carrot, peeled and chopped

2 teaspoons dried oregano

2 teaspoons dried thyme

⅛ teaspoon ground red pepper

1 cup uncooked long-grain
    white rice

Smoked Sausage Gumbo

Slow Cooker Directions

Combine broth and tomatoes in slow cooker. Sprinkle flour evenly over bottom of small skillet. Cook over high heat without stirring 3 to 4 minutes or until flour begins to brown. Reduce heat to medium; stir flour about 4 minutes. Stir in oil until smooth. Carefully whisk flour mixture into slow cooker.

Add sausage, onion, bell pepper, celery, carrot, oregano, thyme and ground red pepper to slow cooker. Stir well. Cover and cook on LOW 4 ½ to 5 hours or until juices are thickened.

About 30 minutes before gumbo is ready to serve, prepare rice. Cook rice in 2 cups boiling water in medium saucepan. Serve gumbo over rice. *Makes 4 servings*

*Quick*Tip

If gumbo thickens upon standing, stir in additional broth. For a special touch, sprinkle chopped parsley over each serving.

Smoked Sausage Gumbo

Ham and Navy Bean Soup

8 ounces dried navy beans, rinsed and drained

6 cups water

1 ham bone

1 medium yellow onion, chopped

2 celery stalks, finely chopped

2 bay leaves

1½ teaspoons dried tarragon leaves

1½ teaspoons salt

¼ teaspoon black pepper

1. Place beans in large bowl; cover completely with water. Soak 6 to 8 hours or overnight. Drain beans; discard water.

2. Combine beans, 6 cups water, ham bone, onion, celery, bay leaves and tarragon in slow cooker. Cook on LOW 8 hours or on HIGH 4 hours. Discard ham bone and bay leaves; stir in salt and pepper. *Makes 8 servings*

318

90's-Style Slow Cooker Coq Au Vin

2 packages BUTTERBALL® Boneless Skinless Chicken Breast Fillets

1 pound fresh mushrooms, sliced thick

1 jar (15 ounces) pearl onions, drained

½ cup dry white wine

1 teaspoon thyme leaves

1 bay leaf

1 cup chicken broth

⅓ cup flour

½ cup chopped fresh parsley

Slow Cooker Directions

Place chicken, mushrooms, onions, wine, thyme and bay leaf into slow cooker. Combine chicken broth and flour; pour into slow cooker. Cover and cook 5 hours on LOW setting. Add parsley. Serve over wild rice pilaf, if desired.

Makes 8 servings

Prep Time: 30 minutes plus cooking time

Middle Eastern Lamb Stew

1½ pounds lamb stew meat, cubed

2 tablespoons all-purpose flour

1 tablespoon vegetable oil

1½ cups beef broth

1 cup chopped onion

½ cup chopped carrots

1 clove garlic, minced

1 tablespoon tomato paste

½ teaspoon ground cumin

½ teaspoon red pepper flakes

¼ teaspoon ground cinnamon

½ cup chopped dried apricots

1 teaspoon salt

¼ teaspoon black pepper

3 cups hot cooked noodles

Slow Cooker Directions

1. Coat lamb with flour; set aside. Heat oil in large nonstick skillet over medium-high heat until hot. Brown half of lamb and transfer to slow cooker; repeat with remaining lamb. Add broth, onion, carrots, garlic, tomato paste, cumin, red pepper and cinnamon. Cover and cook on LOW 3 hours.

2. Stir in apricots, salt and pepper. Cover and cook on LOW 2 to 3 hours, or until lamb is tender and sauce is thickened. Serve lamb over noodles. *Makes 6 servings*

319

HEARTY soups & stews

320

2   small sweet potatoes, peeled and
    cut into 2-inch pieces (about
    12 ounces total)

1   package (10 ounces) frozen corn

1   package (9 ounces) frozen cut
    green beans

1   cup chopped onion

1¼ pounds lean pork stew meat, cut
    into 1-inch cubes

1   can (14½ ounces) diced
    tomatoes

1   to 2 tablespoons chili powder

½   teaspoon salt

½   teaspoon ground coriander

Panama Pork Stew

Place potatoes, corn, green beans and onion in slow cooker.
Top with pork. Stir together tomatoes, 1 cup water, chili
powder, salt and coriander in large bowl. Pour over pork in
slow cooker. Cover and cook on LOW 7 to 9 hours.

Makes 6 servings

Panama Pork Stew

1   tablespoon vegetable oil

1   cup finely chopped onion

1   cup chopped red bell pepper

2   tablespoons minced jalapeño
    pepper

1   clove garlic, minced

1   can (28 ounces) crushed
    tomatoes

1   can (14½ ounces) black beans,
    rinsed and drained

1   can (14 ounces) garbanzo beans,
    drained

½   cup canned corn

¼   cup tomato paste

1   teaspoon sugar

1   teaspoon ground cumin

1   teaspoon dried basil leaves

1   teaspoon chili powder

¼   teaspoon black pepper

1   cup shredded Cheddar cheese
    (optional)

    Sour cream (optional)

Vegetarian Chili

1. Heat oil in large nonstick skillet over medium-high heat until hot. Add chopped onion, bell pepper, jalapeño pepper and garlic; cook and stir 5 minutes or until vegetables are tender.

2. Spoon vegetables into slow cooker. Add remaining ingredients, except cheese, to slow cooker; mix well. Cover and cook on LOW 4 to 5 hours. Garnish with cheese and sour cream, if desired.   *Makes 4 servings*

*Quick*Tip

Omit the optional cheese and sour cream and this chili can satisfy vegan diets, too.

Vegetarian Chili

Oniony Braised Short Ribs

2	tablespoons olive or vegetable oil
3	pounds beef chuck short ribs
1	envelope LIPTON® RECIPE SECRETS® Onion Soup Mix
3¼	cups water
¼	cup ketchup
2	tablespoons firmly packed brown sugar
2	tablespoons sherry (optional)
½	teaspoon ground ginger
1	tablespoon all-purpose flour
¼	cup water
¼	teaspoon ground black pepper

1. In 6-quart Dutch oven or stockpot, heat oil over medium-high heat and brown short ribs in two batches. Return ribs to Dutch oven.

2. Stir in soup mix combined with 3¼ cups water, ketchup, brown sugar, sherry and ginger. Bring to a boil. Reduce heat to low and simmer covered 2 hours or until ribs are tender.

3. Remove ribs to serving platter and keep warm. In Dutch oven, add flour combined with ¼ cup water and pepper. Bring to a boil over high heat. Boil, stirring occasionally, 2 minutes or until thickened. Pour sauce over ribs. Serve, if desired, with crusty bread. *Makes 4 servings*

Slow Cooker Method: Place short ribs in slow cooker. Combine 2½ cups water with soup mix, ketchup, brown sugar, sherry and ginger. Pour over ribs. Cover. Cook on LOW 8 to 10 hours or until ribs are tender. Remove ribs to serving platter. Stir ¼ cup water with flour and black pepper into juices in slow cooker. Cover and cook on HIGH 15 minutes or until thickened. Pour over ribs. Serve as above.

Prep Time: 10 minutes
Cook Time: 2 hours 15 minutes

Black and White Chili

Nonstick cooking spray

1 pound chicken tenders, cut into
   ³/₄-inch pieces

1 cup coarsely chopped onion

1 can (15¹/₂ ounces) Great
   Northern beans, drained

1 can (15 ounces) black beans,
   drained

1 can (14¹/₂ ounces) Mexican-style
   stewed tomatoes, undrained

2 tablespoons Texas-style chili
   powder seasoning mix

Slow Cooker Directions

Spray large saucepan with cooking spray; heat over medium heat until hot. Add chicken and onion; cook and stir 5 minutes or until chicken is browned.

Combine cooked chicken, onion, beans, tomatoes and chili seasoning in slow cooker. Cover and cook on LOW 4 to 4¹/₂ hours.   *Makes 6 (1-cup) servings*

Serving Suggestion: For a change of pace, this delicious chili is excellent served over cooked rice or pasta.

Irish Stew

1 cup fat-free reduced-sodium
   chicken broth

1 teaspoon *each* dried marjoram
   and dried parsley

³/₄ teaspoon salt

¹/₂ teaspoon garlic powder

¹/₄ teaspoon black pepper

1¹/₄ pounds white potatoes, peeled
   and cut into 1-inch pieces

1 pound lean lamb stew meat, cut
   into 1-inch cubes

8 ounces frozen cut green beans

2 small leeks, cut lengthwise into
   halves then crosswise into slices

1¹/₂ cups coarsely chopped carrots

Slow Cooker Directions

Combine broth, marjoram, parsley, salt, garlic powder and pepper in large bowl; mix well. Pour mixture into slow cooker. Add potatoes, lamb, green beans, leeks and carrots. Cover and cook on LOW for 7 to 9 hours.

Makes 6 servings

325

HEARTY *soups & stews*

*If you're the type that likes to get **every last bit** of a delicious soup or stew, then try these breads. They're perfect for **mopping up** all the good stuff or **dunking in** your favorite bowl of chili.*

326

Potato Rosemary Rolls

Dough

- 1 cup plus 2 tablespoons water (70 to 80°F)
- 2 tablespoons olive oil
- 1 teaspoon salt
- 3 cups bread flour
- ½ cup instant potato flakes or buds
- 2 tablespoons nonfat dry milk powder
- 1 tablespoon sugar
- 1 teaspoon SPICE ISLANDS® Rosemary, crushed
- 1½ teaspoons FLEISCHMANN'S® Bread Machine Yeast

Topping

- 1 egg, lightly beaten

  Sesame or poppy seed or additional dried rosemary, crushed

Measure all dough ingredients into bread machine pan in the order suggested by manufacturer, adding potato flakes with flour. Select dough/manual cycle. When cycle is complete, remove dough to floured surface. If necessary, knead in additional flour to make dough easy to handle.

Divide dough into 12 equal pieces. Roll each piece into 10-inch rope; coil each rope and tuck end under coil. Place rolls 2 inches apart on large greased baking sheet. Cover; let rise in warm, draft-free place until doubled in size, about 45 to 60 minutes. Brush tops with beaten egg; sprinkle with sesame seed. Bake at 375°F for 15 to 20 minutes or until done. Remove from pan; cool on wire rack. *Makes 12 rolls*

Note: Dough can be prepared in 1½ and 2-pound bread machines.

Potato Rosemary Rolls

HEARTY soups & steus

2 cups all-purpose flour

1 tablespoon baking powder

½ teaspoon salt

¼ cup vegetable shortening

1 tablespoon grated orange peel

1 tablespoon grated lemon peel

¾ cup mashed cooked sweet potato
(1 large sweet potato baked
until tender, peeled and
mashed)

⅓ cup honey

½ cup milk (about)

328

Honey Sweet Potato Biscuits

Combine flour, baking powder and salt in large bowl. Cut in shortening until mixture resembles size of small peas. Add orange and lemon peels, sweet potato and honey; mix well. Add enough milk to make soft, but not sticky dough. Knead 3 or 4 times on lightly floured surface. Pat dough to 1-inch thickness and cut into 2¼-inch rounds. Place on ungreased baking sheet.

Bake in preheated 400°F oven 15 to 18 minutes or until lightly browned. Serve warm.   *Makes 10 biscuits*

Favorite recipe from **National Honey Board**

Honey Sweet Potato Biscuits

1¼ cups water

1 teaspoon salt

1½ teaspoons sugar

3 tablespoons white cornmeal

3¾ cups bread flour

2¼ teaspoons RED STAR® Active Dry Yeast

Bread Bowls

Bread Machine Method

Place room temperature ingredients in pan in order listed. Select dough cycle. At end of cycle, remove dough; follow shaping and baking instructions.

Traditional Method

Combine yeast, 1 cup flour and other dry ingredients. Heat water to 120° to 130°F; add to flour mixture. Beat 3 minutes on medium speed. By hand, stir in enough remaining flour to make firm dough. Knead on floured surface 5 to 7 minutes until smooth and elastic. Use additional flour, if necessary. Place dough in lightly greased bowl. Cover; let rise until dough tests ripe.*

Shaping

Turn dough onto lightly floured surface; punch down to remove air bubbles. Divide and shape into three round balls. Place on greased cookie sheet covered with cornmeal. Cover; let rise until indentation remains after lightly touching sides of bowls. Bake in preheated 425°F oven 20 to 30 minutes. Spray or brush loaf with cold water several times during first 10 minutes of baking for a crisper crust. Remove from cookie sheet; cool.

To Make Bowls

Cut a thin slice off the top. Hollow out inside, leaving half-inch sides. Placing bowls in a 300°F oven for 10 minutes will dry sides and prevent premature soaking from salads and soups. *Makes 3 bread bowls*

*Place two fingers into dough and then remove them. If the holes remain, the dough is ripe and ready to punch down.

Bread Bowls

¼ cup chopped red bell pepper

¼ cup chopped green bell pepper

2 small jalapeño peppers,* minced

2 cloves garlic, minced

¾ cup corn

1½ cups yellow cornmeal

½ cup all-purpose flour

2 tablespoons sugar

2 teaspoons baking powder

½ teaspoon baking soda

½ teaspoon ground cumin

½ teaspoon salt

1½ cups buttermilk

1 whole egg

2 egg whites

4 tablespoons margarine, melted

*Jalapeño peppers can sting and irritate the skin; wear rubber gloves when handling peppers and do not touch eyes. Wash hands after handling.

Chili Cornbread

1. **PREHEAT** oven to 425°F. Spray 8×8-inch square baking pan with nonstick cooking spray. Set aside.

2. **SPRAY** small skillet with nonstick cooking spray. Add bell and jalapeño peppers and garlic; cook and stir 3 to 4 minutes or until peppers are tender. Stir in corn; cook 1 to 2 minutes. Remove from heat.

3. **COMBINE** cornmeal, flour, sugar, baking powder, baking soda, cumin and salt in large bowl. Add buttermilk, whole egg, egg whites and margarine; mix until smooth. Stir in corn mixture.

4. **POUR** batter into prepared baking pan. Bake 25 to 30 minutes or until golden brown. Cool on wire rack.

Makes 12 servings

Chili Cornbread

Mexican Bubble Rolls

2	cups warm water (100°F to 110°F), divided
2	envelopes FLEISCHMANN'S® Active Dry Yeast
¼	cup sugar
¼	cup butter or margarine, softened
1	tablespoon salt
4	to 4½ cups all-purpose flour, divided
1½	cups yellow cornmeal
2	jars (4 ounces each) diced pimientos, well-drained
¾	cup grated Parmesan cheese
1	tablespoon whole cumin seed, toasted

Place ½ cup warm water in large warm bowl. Sprinkle in yeast; stir until dissolved. Add remaining 1½ cups water, sugar, butter, salt, 1½ cups flour and cornmeal; blend well. Beat 2 minutes at medium speed of electric mixer, scraping bowl occasionally. Add 1 cup flour; beat 2 minutes at high speed. Stir in enough remaining flour to make a soft dough. Knead on a floured surface until smooth, about 8 to 10 minutes. Place in a greased bowl, turning to grease top. Cover; let rise in a warm, draft-free place until doubled in size, about 1 hour. Meanwhile, combine pimientos, cheese and cumin seed in small bowl. Mix well. Punch dough down. On floured surface, divide dough into 24 pieces; flatten to 3-inch circles. Place 2 teaspoons pimiento mixture in center of each circle. Pull up dough to enclose filling and pinch to seal. Place balls, sealed side down, in 2 greased 9-inch round cake pans.* Cover; let rise in a warm, draft-free place until doubled in size, about 30 minutes. Bake at 375°F for 25 minutes or until done. Remove from pans; cool on wire racks.

Makes 24 rolls

Two 10-cup tube pans may be used. Bake at 375°F for 30 minutes or until done.

Mexican Bubble Rolls

Angel Biscuits

⅓ cup warm water (110°F)

1 package (¼ ounce) active dry yeast

5 cups all-purpose flour

3 tablespoons sugar

1 tablespoon baking powder

1 teaspoon baking soda

1 teaspoon salt

1 cup shortening

2 cups buttermilk

Preheat oven to 450°F. Pour warm water into small bowl. Sprinkle yeast over water and stir until dissolved. Let stand 10 minutes or until small bubbles form.

Combine flour, sugar, baking powder, baking soda and salt in large bowl. Add shortening. With fingers, pastry blender or 2 knives, rub or cut in shortening until mixture resembles fine crumbs. Make a well in center. Pour in yeast mixture and buttermilk; stir with fork until mixture forms dough.

Turn dough out onto lightly floured board. Knead 30 seconds or until dough feels light and soft but not sticky. Roll out desired amount of dough to ½-inch thickness. Cut biscuit rounds with 2-inch cutter. Place biscuits close together (for soft sides) or ½ inch apart (for crispy sides) on ungreased baking sheet. Bake 15 to 18 minutes or until tops are lightly browned.

Place remaining dough in airtight bag; refrigerate up to 3 days. Or roll out and cut remaining dough into rounds; place on baking sheet and freeze. Transfer frozen rounds to airtight bags; return to freezer. At baking time, place frozen rounds on ungreased baking sheet. Let stand 20 minutes or until thawed before baking. Bake as directed.

Makes about 5 dozen biscuits

Red Devil Biscuits: Prepare Angel Biscuits but add 2 tablespoons mild red chili powder to flour mixture. Cut biscuits regular size to serve as a hot bread. To serve as an appetizer, cut biscuits miniature size. Serve with your favorite cheese spread or with softened butter and thinly sliced roast beef or turkey.

Beer Batter Rye Bread

2 cups all-purpose flour, divided

½ cup rye flour

2 tablespoons molasses or packed brown sugar

2 tablespoons vegetable oil

1 tablespoon caraway seeds

1 package (¼ ounce) active dry yeast

1 teaspoon salt

1 cup beer

1. Fit processor with steel blade. Add 1 cup all-purpose flour, rye flour, molasses, oil, caraway seeds, yeast and salt into work bowl. Process until mixed, about 5 seconds.

2. Heat beer in small saucepan over low heat until 120° to 130°F. Turn on processor and add beer all at once through feed tube. Process until blended, about 30 seconds. Turn on processor and add remaining 1 cup flour, ¼ cup at a time, through feed tube. Process 5 to 10 seconds after each addition. (If food processor sounds strained and/or motor slows down or stops, turn off processor immediately and stir any remaining flour into batter by hand.)

3. Pour batter into greased 1½-quart baking dish. Let stand in warm place (85°F) until almost doubled, about 45 minutes.

4. Heat oven to 350°F. Bake until wooden pick inserted in center comes out clean, about 30 minutes. Cool 10 minutes. Remove bread from baking dish and cool on wire rack.

Makes 1 loaf

337

HEARTY soups & stews

Crispie Cheese Twists

1/2 cup grated Parmesan cheese

3/4 teaspoon LAWRY'S® Seasoned Pepper

1/2 teaspoon LAWRY'S® Garlic Powder with Parsley

1 package (17 3/4 ounces) frozen puff pastry, thawed

1 egg white, lightly beaten

Preheat oven to 350°F. In small bowl, combine Parmesan cheese, Seasoned Pepper and Garlic Powder with Parsley. Unfold pastry sheets onto cutting board. Brush pastry lightly with egg white; sprinkle each sheet with 1/4 of the cheese mixture. Lightly press into pastry; turn over and repeat. Cut each sheet into 12 (1-inch-wide) strips; twist. Place on greased cookie sheet. Bake 15 minutes or until golden brown.
Makes 2 dozen twists

Serving Suggestion: Serve in a napkin-lined basket. Place layer of plastic wrap over napkin to protect it.

338

Thyme-Cheese Bubble Loaf

1 cup water

2 tablespoons vegetable oil

1 teaspoon salt

3 cups all-purpose flour

1 cup (4 ounces) shredded Monterey Jack cheese

1 teaspoon sugar

1 1/2 teaspoons active dry yeast

1/4 cup chopped fresh parsley

3 teaspoons finely chopped fresh thyme *or* 3/4 teaspoon dried thyme leaves, crushed

1/4 cup butter, melted

Place first seven ingredients in bread machine pan in order specified by owner's manual. Program dough cycle setting; press start. Combine parsley and thyme in shallow bowl; set aside. Lightly grease 8 1/2×4 1/2-inch loaf pan or 1 1/2-quart casserole dish; set aside. When cycle is complete, remove dough to lightly floured surface. If necessary, knead in additional all-purpose flour to make dough easy to handle. Divide dough into 48 equal pieces, shape each into smooth ball, dip into melted butter and herb mixture, and place in prepared pan in two evenly spaced layers. Cover with clean towel; let rise in warm, draft-free place 45 minutes or until doubled in size. Preheat oven to 375°F. Bake 25 to 35 minutes or until golden brown. Remove from pan; cool on wire rack.
Makes 1 (1 1/2-pound) loaf

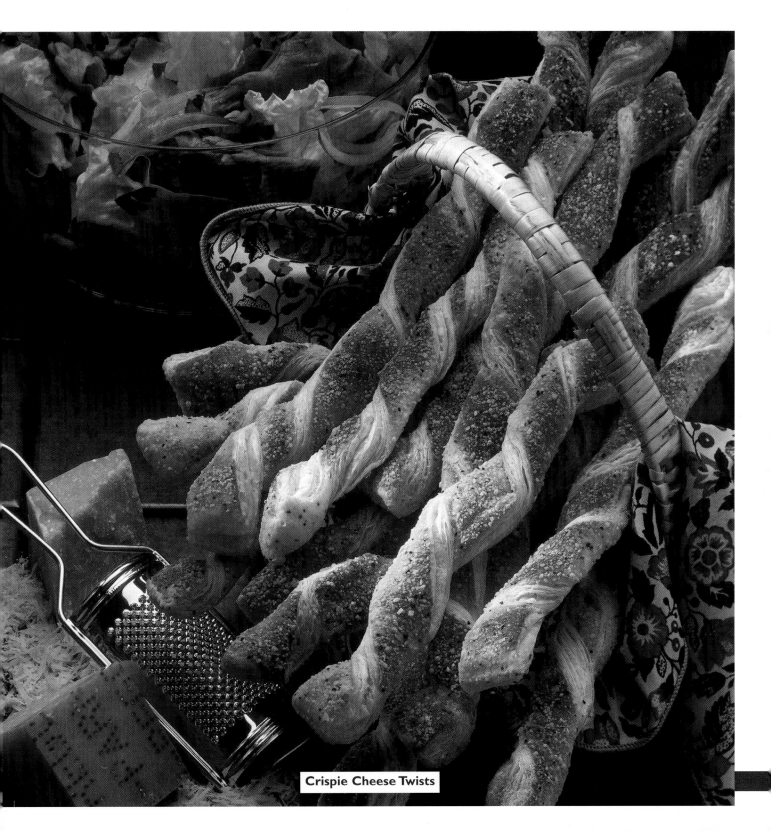

Crispie Cheese Twists

Sage Buns

1½   cups milk

2   tablespoons shortening

3   to 4 cups all-purpose flour, divided

2   tablespoons sugar

1   package active dry yeast

2   teaspoons rubbed sage

1   teaspoon salt

1   tablespoon olive oil (optional)

1. Heat milk and shortening in small saucepan over medium heat, stirring constantly, until shortening is melted and temperature reaches 120° to 130°F. Remove from heat. Grease 13×9-inch pan; set aside.

2. Combine 2 cups flour, sugar, yeast, sage and salt in large bowl. Add milk mixture; beat vigorously 2 minutes. Add remaining flour, ¼ cup at a time, until dough begins to pull away from sides of bowl.

3. Turn out dough onto floured work surface; flatten slightly. Knead 10 minutes or until dough is smooth and elastic, adding flour if necessary to prevent sticking.

4. Shape dough into ball. Place in large lightly oiled bowl; turn dough over once to oil surface. Cover with towel; let rise in warm place 1 hour or until doubled in bulk.

5. Turn out dough onto lightly oiled surface. Divide into 24 equal pieces. Form each piece into ball. Place evenly spaced in prepared pan. Cover with towel; let rise 45 minutes.

6. Preheat oven to 375°F. Bake 15 to 20 minutes or until golden brown. Immediately remove bread from pan and cool on wire rack. Brush tops of rolls with olive oil for soft shiny tops, if desired. *Makes 24 rolls*

Sage Buns

Celestial Crackers

Ingredients

1	cup all-purpose flour
1/2	teaspoon baking powder
1/2	teaspoon paprika
1/4	teaspoon salt
1/3	cup plus 1 tablespoon water, divided
3	tablespoons vegetable oil
1	egg white
	Toppings: sesame seeds, poppy seeds, garlic salt and dried herbs

Supplies

	2-inch star- and moon-shaped cookie cutters

1. Combine flour, baking powder, paprika and salt in medium bowl. Stir in 1/3 cup water and oil to form smooth dough.

2. Preheat oven to 400°F. Grease baking sheets.

3. Roll dough on floured surface to 14×12-inch rectangle. Cut dough into star and moon shapes using cutters. Place on prepared baking sheets.

4. Combine egg white and 1 tablespoon water; brush on crackers. Sprinkle with toppings.

5. Bake 8 to 10 minutes until edges begin to brown. Remove to wire rack; cool completely.   *Makes 2½ dozen*

Lickety-Split Beer Rolls

WESSON® No-Stick Cooking
  Spray
4 cups self-rising flour
¼ cup sugar
1 teaspoon salt
2 cups beer
½ cup WESSON® Canola Oil
1½ tablespoons caraway seeds

Preheat oven to 400°F. Spray muffin cups with Wesson Cooking Spray. In a large mixing bowl, combine flour, sugar and salt; blend well. Add beer and Wesson Oil; stir until dry ingredients are moistened. Fold in caraway seeds. Fill muffin cups to rim with batter; bake 30 to 35 minutes or until tops are golden brown. Cool for 5 minutes. Remove rolls from pan; cool on wire rack. Serve warm or cool.

Makes 1½ dozen rolls

Barbecued French Bread

2 tablespoons butter
⅓ cup chopped onion
½ clove garlic, minced
⅓ cup chili sauce
2 tablespoons vinegar
1 tablespoon brown sugar
1 tablespoon prepared mustard
1½ teaspoons TABASCO® brand
  Pepper Sauce
1 large loaf French bread
  Grated Parmesan cheese

Preheat oven to 400°F. Melt butter in medium saucepan over medium heat. Add onion and garlic; cook and stir about 3 minutes. Stir in chili sauce, vinegar, brown sugar, mustard and TABASCO® Sauce; simmer about 5 minutes or until mixture thickens.

Cut French bread diagonally into ¾-inch slices, almost but not through to bottom of loaf. Spread sauce between slices; sprinkle with Parmesan cheese. Wrap in aluminum foil and heat in oven 15 minutes.

Makes 1 loaf

343

HEARTY soups & stews

1 cup milk

1 egg

2 tablespoons butter, softened

1¼ teaspoons salt

2⅓ cups bread flour

⅔ cup cornmeal

1 tablespoon sugar

½ teaspoon white pepper

½ teaspoon dried oregano leaves

1½ teaspoons active dry yeast

1 cup prepared chunky salsa

Salsa Corn Bread Twists

1. Measuring carefully, place all ingredients except salsa in bread machine pan in order specified by owner's manual. Program dough cycle setting; press start. (Do not use delay cycle.) Drain liquid from salsa. Pat salsa dry with paper towel and set aside.

2. When cycle is complete, remove dough to lightly floured surface. (Dough will be soft.) If necessary, knead in additional bread flour to make dough easy to handle. Roll dough into 16×10-inch rectangle; spread with salsa. Fold dough in half into 16×5-inch rectangle; pinch edges to seal. With sharp knife, evenly slice into 9 (5×1½-inch) strips.

3. Lightly dust baking sheets with additional cornmeal. Gently twist each strip several times; place on prepared baking sheet. Cover with clean towel; let rise in warm, draft-free place 45 minutes or until doubled in size.

4. Preheat oven to 350°F. Bake twists 20 to 25 minutes or until golden brown. Remove from baking sheets; cool on wire racks.

Makes 9 twists

Salsa Corn Bread Twists

1½-Pound Loaf

¾	cup water
¼	cup molasses
2	tablespoons butter, softened
1	teaspoon salt
2½	cups all-purpose flour
½	cup yellow cornmeal
1½	teaspoons active dry yeast

2-Pound Loaf

1	cup water
⅓	cup molasses
3	tablespoons butter, softened
1½	teaspoons salt
3¼	cups all-purpose flour
¾	cup yellow cornmeal
2	teaspoons active dry yeast

Anadama Bread

1. Measuring carefully, place all ingredients in bread machine pan in order specified by owner's manual.

2. Program basic cycle and desired crust setting; press start. Immediately remove baked bread from pan; cool on wire rack.

Variation: Follow instructions through Step 1. Program dough cycle setting instead of basic cycle; press start. For 1½-pound loaf, grease 1-quart soufflé or casserole dish; set aside. For 2-pound loaf, grease 1½-quart soufflé or casserole dish; set aside. When cycle is complete, remove dough to lightly floured surface. If necessary, knead in additional all-purpose flour to make dough easy to handle. Shape dough into smooth ball and place in prepared dish. Cover dough with clean towel; let rise in warm, draft-free place 45 minutes or until doubled in size. Preheat oven to 375°F. Bake 25 to 35 minutes or until loaf is browned and sounds hollow when tapped. Remove from pan; cool on wire rack.

THE HISTORY OF **BREAD** DATES AS FAR BACK AS THE **EGYPTIANS,** WHO FIRST DISCOVERED LEAVEN BY ACCIDENTALLY PREPARING BREAD FROM SOURED DOUGH. FROM THERE, BREAD BECAME A STAPLE IN THE DIETS OF MANY. THE **HEBREWS** BROUGHT UNLEAVENED BREAD AS THEY CROSSED THE **RED SEA**, THE GREEKS AND ROMANS COOKED THEIR LEAVENED LOAVES IN OVENS, WHILE THE **GAULS** USED BEER AS A LEAVENING AGENT. SANTÉ!

347

HEARTY soups & stews

2 cups all-purpose flour

4 tablespoons grated Parmesan cheese, divided

1 tablespoon baking powder

$^1\!/_2$ teaspoon baking soda

$^1\!/_4$ teaspoon salt (optional)

4 tablespoons Neufchâtel cheese

2 tablespoons margarine, divided

6 ounces plain nonfat yogurt

$^1\!/_3$ cup slivered fresh basil leaves

Basil Biscuits

1. Combine flour, 2 tablespoons Parmesan, baking powder, baking soda and salt in large bowl. Cut in Neufchâtel and 1 tablespoon margarine with pastry blender or two knives until mixture forms coarse crumbs. Stir in yogurt and basil, mixing just until dough clings together. Turn dough out onto lightly floured surface and gently pat into ball. Knead just until dough holds together. Pat and roll dough into 7-inch log. Cut into 7 (1-inch-thick) slices.

2. Spray 10-inch cast iron skillet or Dutch oven with nonstick cooking spray; arrange biscuits in skillet. Melt remaining 1 tablespoon margarine and brush over biscuit tops. Sprinkle with remaining 2 tablespoons Parmesan. Place skillet on grid set 4 to 6 inches above medium-hot coals (about 375°F); cover grill. Bake 20 to 40 minutes or until golden and firm on top. *Makes 7 biscuits*

Note: To prepare a charcoal grill for baking, arrange a single, solid, even layer of medium coals in bottom of charcoal grill. If necessary, reduce temperature by either allowing coals to cook down or removing 3 or 4 coals at a time to a fireproof container until desired temperature is reached. For a gas grill, begin on medium heat and adjust heat as necessary. Besides raising or lowering the temperature setting, you can turn off one side of the grill or set each side to a different temperature.

Basil Biscuits

HEARTY soups & stews

350

1 large head garlic (about 14 to 16 cloves)

3 tablespoons olive oil, divided

3 tablespoons water, divided

1 tablespoon butter or margarine, softened

1 package active dry yeast

1 teaspoon sugar

1 cup warm water (105° to 115°F)

2½ to 3 cups all-purpose flour, divided

1 teaspoon salt

1 egg white

1 tablespoon sesame seeds

Roasted Garlic Breadsticks

1. Preheat oven to 350°F. Remove outer papery skin from garlic head. Place garlic in 10-ounce ovenproof custard cup. Drizzle with 1 tablespoon olive oil and 2 tablespoons water. Cover tightly with foil. Bake 1 hour or until garlic cloves are tender. Remove foil and let cool. When cool, break into cloves. Squeeze garlic out, finely chop and combine with butter in small bowl. Cover; set aside.

2. Sprinkle yeast and sugar over 1 cup warm water in large bowl; stir until yeast dissolves. Let stand 5 minutes or until bubbly. Beat 1½ cups flour, salt and remaining 2 tablespoons olive oil into yeast mixture with electric mixer at low speed until blended, scraping down side of bowl once. Increase speed to medium; beat 2 minutes. Stir in enough additional flour, about 1 cup, with wooden spoon to make soft dough.

3. Turn out dough onto lightly floured surface; flatten slightly. Knead dough about 5 minutes or until smooth and elastic, adding remaining ½ cup flour to prevent sticking if necessary. Shape dough into a ball; place in large greased bowl. Turn dough over so that top is greased. Cover with clean kitchen towel; let rise in warm place about 1 hour or until doubled in bulk.

4. Punch down dough. Knead dough on lightly floured surface 1 minute. Cover with towel; let rest 10 minutes. Grease 2 large baking sheets; set aside. Roll dough into 12-inch square with lightly floured rolling pin; spread garlic mixture evenly over it. Fold square in half.

continued on page 352

Roasted Garlic Breadsticks

continued from page 350

5. Roll dough into 14×7-inch rectangle; cut crosswise into 7×1-inch strips. Holding ends of each strip, twist 3 to 4 times; place strips 2 inches apart on prepared baking sheets, pressing both ends to seal. Cover with clean kitchen towels; let rise in warm place about 30 minutes or until doubled in bulk.

6. Preheat oven to 400°F. Combine egg white and remaining 1 tablespoon water in small bowl. Brush sticks with egg white mixture; sprinkle with sesame seeds. Bake 20 to 22 minutes or until golden. Serve warm.   *Makes 12 bread sticks*

Rosemary Breadsticks

²/₃	cup reduced-fat (2%) milk
¹/₄	cup finely chopped fresh chives
2	teaspoons baking powder
1	teaspoon finely chopped fresh rosemary or dried rosemary
³/₄	teaspoon salt
¹/₂	teaspoon black pepper
³/₄	cup whole wheat flour
³/₄	cup all-purpose flour
	Nonstick cooking spray

1. Combine milk, chives, baking powder, rosemary, salt and pepper in large bowl; mix well. Stir in flours, ¹/₂ cup at a time, until blended. Turn onto floured surface and knead dough about 5 minutes or until smooth and elastic, adding more flour if dough is sticky. Let stand 30 minutes at room temperature.

2. Preheat oven to 375°F. Spray baking sheet with cooking spray. Divide dough into 12 balls, about 1¹/₄ ounces each. Roll each ball into long thin rope; place on prepared baking sheet. Lightly spray breadsticks with cooking spray. Bake about 12 minutes or until bottoms are golden brown. Turn breadsticks over; bake about 10 minutes more or until golden brown.

Makes 12 breadsticks

Herb Corn Bread

1-pound loaf

- ½ cup water
- ½ cup evaporated milk
- 2 tablespoons vegetable oil
- Pinch dried sweet marjoram
- Pinch ground ginger
- ¾ teaspoon celery seed
- ¾ teaspoon dried sage
- 1 teaspoon salt
- 2 tablespoons sugar
- ¼ cup yellow cornmeal
- 2¼ cups bread flour
- 1½ teaspoons RED STAR® Active Dry Yeast

2-pound loaf

- ½ cup plus 2 tablespoons water
- 1 cup evaporated milk
- ¼ cup vegetable oil
- ¼ teaspoon dried sweet marjoram
- ¼ teaspoon ground ginger
- 1¼ teaspoons celery seed
- 1¼ teaspoons dried sage
- 2 teaspoons salt
- ¼ cup sugar
- ½ cup yellow cornmeal
- 4 cups bread flour
- 1 tablespoon RED STAR® Active Dry Yeast

Bread Machine Method

Have liquid ingredients at 80°F and all others at room temperature. Place ingredients in pan in order listed. Select basic cycle and medium/normal crust. Do not use delay timer.

Hand-Held Mixer Method

Combine dry mixture and liquid ingredients in mixing bowl on low speed. Beat 2 to 3 minutes on medium speed. Stir in enough remaining flour by hand to make firm dough. Knead on floured surface 5 to 7 minutes until smooth and elastic. Use additional flour if necessary.

Stand Mixer Method

Combine dry mixture and liquid ingredients in mixing bowl with paddle or beaters for 4 minutes on medium speed. Gradually add remaining flour and knead with dough hooks 5 to 7 minutes until smooth and elastic.

Rising, Shaping, and Baking

Place dough in lightly oiled bowl and turn to grease top. Cover; let rise until dough tests ripe.* Turn dough onto lightly floured surface; punch down to remove air bubbles. Roll or pat into a 14×7-inch rectangle. Starting with shorter side, roll up tightly, pressing dough into roll. Pinch edges and ends to seal. Place in greased 9×5-inch loaf pan. Cover; let rise until indentation remains after touching dough. Bake in preheated 375°F oven 30 to 40 minutes. Remove from pan; cool.

Makes 1 loaf

Stick two fingers into dough and then remove them. If the holes remain, the dough is ripe and ready to punch down.

353

HEARTY soups & stews

Pull-Apart Rye Rolls

³/₄ cup water

2 tablespoons margarine or butter, softened

2 tablespoons molasses

2¹/₄ cups all-purpose flour, divided

¹/₂ cup rye flour

¹/₃ cup nonfat dry milk powder

1 package active dry yeast

1¹/₂ teaspoons salt

1¹/₂ teaspoons caraway seeds

Melted margarine or vegetable oil

Heat water, softened margarine and molasses in small saucepan over low heat until temperature reaches 120° to 130°F. Combine 1¹/₄ cups all-purpose flour, rye flour, milk powder, yeast, salt and caraway seeds in large bowl. Stir heated water mixture into flour mixture with wooden spoon to form soft but sticky dough. Gradually add more all-purpose flour until rough dough forms.

Turn out dough onto lightly floured surface. Knead 5 to 8 minutes or until smooth and elastic, gradually adding remaining flour to prevent sticking, if necessary. Cover with inverted bowl. Let rise 35 to 40 minutes or until dough has increased in bulk by one third. Punch down dough; divide into halves. Roll each half into 12-inch log. Cut each log evenly into 12 pieces using sharp knife; shape into tight balls. Arrange in greased 8- or 9-inch cake pan. Brush tops with melted margarine. Loosely cover with lightly greased sheet of plastic wrap. Let rise in warm place 45 minutes or until doubled in bulk.

Preheat oven to 375°F. Uncover rolls; bake 15 to 20 minutes or until golden brown. Cool in pan on wire rack 5 minutes. Remove from pan. Cool completely on wire rack.

Makes 24 rolls

Pull-Apart Rye Rolls

4 ounces Emmenthaler Swiss, Gruyère, sharp Cheddar or Swiss cheese

3 to 6 tablespoons warm water (105° to 115°F)

1 package (¼ ounce) active dry yeast

1 teaspoon sugar

2½ cups all-purpose flour

¼ cup butter or margarine, at room temperature

1 teaspoon salt

2 large eggs

Vegetable oil

Gannat (French Cheese Bread)

1. Fit processor with shredding disc. Fit cheese into feed tube, cutting it if necessary. Process until all cheese is shredded. Remove cheese from work bowl and reserve. Combine 3 tablespoons of the water, yeast and sugar. Stir to dissolve yeast and let stand until bubbly, about 5 minutes.

2. Measure flour, butter and salt into processor. With steel blade, process until mixed, about 15 seconds. Add yeast mixture and eggs; process until blended, about 15 seconds. Turn on processor and very slowly drizzle just enough remaining water through feed tube so dough forms a ball that cleans the sides of the bowl. Process until ball turns around bowl about 25 times. Let dough stand 1 to 2 minutes. Turn on processor and gradually drizzle in enough remaining water to make dough soft and smooth but not sticky. Process until dough turns around bowl about 15 times.

3. Turn dough onto lightly floured surface. Shape into ball and place in lightly greased bowl, turning to grease all sides. Cover loosely with plastic wrap and let stand in warm place (85°F) until doubled, about 1 hour. Punch down dough. Place dough on lightly greased surface and knead reserved cheese into dough. Roll or pat into circle 8 inches in diameter. Place in well greased 9-inch round cake or pie pan. Brush with oil. Let stand in warm place until doubled, about 45 minutes.

4. Heat oven to 375°F. Bake until evenly browned and bread sounds hollow when tapped, 30 to 35 minutes. Remove immediately from pan. Cool on wire rack. *Makes 1 loaf*

Poppy Seed Breadsticks

1 cup hot milk (about 120°F)

¼ CRISCO® Stick or 1 cup CRISCO® all-vegetable shortening

1 tablespoon sugar

1 teaspoon salt

1 package active dry yeast

3 to 3½ cups all-purpose flour, divided

1 egg

2 tablespoons water

Poppy seeds

1. Combine milk, ¼ cup shortening, sugar and salt. Cool slightly.

2. Combine yeast and 2½ cups flour in large bowl. Stir in milk mixture until well blended. Beat in enough remaining flour to make a stiff dough.

3. Turn dough onto lightly floured surface. Knead for 5 minutes or until smooth and elastic. Let rest for 5 minutes.

4. Cut dough into 72 equal pieces with sharp knife. Roll out each piece between palms of hands or on flat surface to make a 6-inch strip. Place on greased cookie sheets.

5. Combine egg and water. Brush breadsticks with egg mixture and sprinkle with poppy seeds. Cover; let rest for 20 minutes.

6. Heat oven to 300°F.

7. Bake at 300°F for 45 to 50 minutes or until golden brown. *Do not overbake.* Cool on racks.

Makes 72 breadsticks

357

HEARTY *soups & stews*

4 cups all-purpose flour

$^1/_2$ cup grated Parmesan cheese

2 tablespoons baking powder

2 teaspoons sugar

1 teaspoon baking soda

6 tablespoons cold butter, cut into pieces

6 tablespoons cold solid vegetable shortening

1 cup plus 2 tablespoons buttermilk, divided

$^1/_2$ cup Frank's® RedHot® Cayenne Pepper Sauce

Sesame seeds (optional)

Zesty Parmesan Biscuits

1. Preheat oven to 450°F. Place flour, cheese, baking powder, sugar and baking soda in blender or food processor*. Cover; process 30 seconds. Add butter and shortening; process, pulsing on and off, until fine crumbs form. Transfer to large bowl.

2. Add 1 cup buttermilk and **Frank's RedHot** Sauce all at once. Stir together just until mixture starts to form a ball. (Dough will be dry. Do not over mix.)

3. Turn dough out onto lightly floured board. With palms of hands, gently knead 8 times. Using floured rolling pin or hands, roll dough to ¾-inch thickness. Using 2½-inch round biscuit cutter, cut out 16 biscuits, re-rolling dough as necessary.

4. Place biscuits 2 inches apart on large foil-lined baking sheet. Brush tops with remaining 2 tablespoons buttermilk; sprinkle with sesame seeds, if desired. Bake 12 to 15 minutes or until golden. *Makes 16 biscuits*

Or, place dry ingredients in large bowl. Cut in butter and shortening until fine crumbs form using pastry blender or 2 knives. Add buttermilk and Frank's RedHot Sauce; mix just until moistened. Continue with step 3.

Prep Time: 30 minutes
Cook Time: 12 minutes

Zesty Parmesan Biscuits

1 cup cultured buttermilk
¼ cup water
¼ cup oil
2 tablespoons sugar
1 teaspoon salt
½ teaspoon baking soda
3 cups bread flour
2¼ teaspoons RED STAR® Active Dry Yeast *or* QUICK•RISE™ Yeast

Buttermilk Pan Rolls

Bread Machine Method

Have all ingredients at room temperature. Place ingredients in the pan in the order specified in your owner's manual. Select dough/manual cycle. Do not use the delay timer.

Mixer Methods

Combine yeast, 1 cup flour, and other dry ingredients. Combine buttermilk and oil; heat to 120° to 130°F.

Hand-Held Mixer Method

Combine dry mixture and liquid ingredients in mixing bowl on low speed. Beat 2 to 3 minutes on medium speed. By hand stir in enough remaining flour to make a soft dough. Knead on floured surface until smooth, about 2 minutes.

Stand Mixer Method

Combine dry mixture and liquid ingredients in mixing bowl with paddle or beaters for 4 minutes on medium speed. Gradually add remaining flour and knead with dough hook(s) 5 minutes until smooth.

Shaping and Baking

Press dough evenly into greased 9-inch square cake pan. Sprinkle top of dough lightly with flour. With sharp knife, cut dough into 12 rolls, cutting almost to bottom of pan. Cover; let rise in warm place until indentation remains after touching. Bake in preheated oven 400°F for 15 to 20 minutes until golden brown. Remove from pan. Break apart into rolls; serve warm.

Crusty Rye Bread

¼ cup packed light brown sugar

3 strips pared orange peel

1 cup water

1 tablespoon butter or margarine

1 teaspoon salt

1 teaspoon caraway seeds

2 to 2½ cups all-purpose flour

½ cup rye flour

1 package (¼ ounce) active dry yeast

1. Fit processor with steel blade. Add sugar and orange rind to work bowl. Process until rind is minced, about 1 minute.

2. Place orange mixture in a small saucepan. Add water, butter, salt and caraway seeds. Bring to boil. Remove from heat and cool to 120° to 130°F.

3. Refit processor with steel blade. Measure 1 cup of the all-purpose flour, rye flour and yeast into work bowl. Process on/off twice to mix. Add cooled orange mixture; process until smooth, about 20 seconds.

4. Turn on processor and add enough of the remaining flour through feed tube so dough forms a ball that cleans the sides of the bowl. Process until ball turns around bowl about 25 times.

5. Turn dough onto lightly greased surface. Shape into ball and place in lightly greased bowl, turning to grease all sides. Cover loosely with plastic wrap and let stand in warm place (85°F) until doubled, about 1 hour.

6. Punch down dough. Shape into ball and place on greased cookie sheet. Roll or pat into circle 9 inches in diameter. Cover loosely with plastic wrap and let stand in warm place until almost doubled, about 45 minutes.

7. Heat oven to 350°F. Bake until evenly browned and loaf sounds hollow when tapped, 25 to 30 minutes. Remove from cookie sheet. Cool on wire rack.

Makes 1 loaf

361

HEARTY soups & stews

HEARTY soups & stews

1 cup warm water (105°F to 115°F)

2 envelopes quick-rising dry yeast

¼ teaspoon sugar

⅔ cup whole milk, room temperature

⅓ cup sugar

¼ cup WESSON® Canola Oil

1 large egg

1 tablespoon poppy seeds

2½ teaspoons salt

5⅓ cups all-purpose flour

1 cup (2 sticks) chilled unsalted butter, cut into thin slices

WESSON® No-Stick Cooking Spray

3 tablespoons unsalted butter, melted

Poppy seeds

Fanfare Dinner Rolls

Pour water into a large bowl. Sprinkle yeast, then ¼ teaspoon sugar into water; stir well. Let stand 5 to 8 minutes or until slightly foamy. In a small bowl, whisk milk, ⅓ cup sugar, Wesson Oil, egg, 1 tablespoon poppy seeds and salt until well blended. Pour milk mixture into yeast mixture; mix well. Gradually add 1 cup flour; stir until batter is smooth. In a food processor, combine 4 cups flour and butter; process until mixture resembles coarse meal. Add to batter; stir until moistened. Knead dough in bowl (about 5 minutes) until smooth. Add more flour if dough is sticky. Cover with towels; let rise in warm place for 30 minutes or until nearly doubled in size.

Spray 24 muffin cups with Wesson Cooking Spray. Turn dough onto floured surface; knead about 4 minutes until dough is smooth and elastic. Evenly divide dough into 4 portions. Place 1 portion on floured surface; cover and refrigerate remaining portions. Roll dough to $13 \times 12 \times \frac{1}{8}$-inch rectangle; cut into six 2-inch strips. Stack strips on top of each other to form 6 layers; cut into 6 equal individual small stacks. Place each stack, cut side down, into muffin cup. Repeat with remaining dough sections. Cover with towels; let rise in a warm place for 30 minutes or until nearly doubled in size.

Place one rack in center of oven and the other above with enough space for rolls to rise while baking. Preheat oven to 350°F. Brush rolls gently with melted butter; sprinkle with poppy seeds. Bake 25 minutes until golden brown. Switch muffin pans halfway through bake time. Cool rolls 7 to 10 minutes. Remove from pan; cool on wire rack.   *Makes 2 dozen rolls*

Fanfare Dinner Rolls

English Bath Buns

½ cup warm water (100° to 110°F)

2 envelopes FLEISCHMANN'S® Active Dry Yeast

½ cup warm milk (100° to 110°F)

½ cup butter or margarine, softened

2 tablespoons sugar

1 teaspoon salt

4 cups all-purpose flour, divided

2 large eggs

1 egg, slightly beaten with 1 tablespoon water

¼ cup sugar

1 cup chopped almonds

Place warm water in large warm bowl. Sprinkle in yeast; stir until dissolved. Add warm milk, butter, 2 tablespoons sugar, salt, and 2 cups flour. Beat 2 minutes at medium speed of electric mixer. Add 2 eggs and ½ cup flour. Beat 2 minutes at high speed, scraping bowl occasionally. Stir in enough remaining flour to make soft dough. Knead on lightly floured surface until smooth and elastic, about 10 minutes. Place in greased bowl, turning to grease top. Cover; let rise in warm, draft-free place until doubled in size, about 1 hour.

Punch dough down; turn out onto lightly floured surface. Divide into 24 equal pieces. Shape each piece into smooth balls. Place in greased 2½-inch muffin cups. Cover; let rise in warm, draft-free place until doubled in size, about 30 minutes. Brush tops with egg mixture. Sprinkle ¼ cup sugar and almonds over tops. Bake at 375°F for 20 minutes or until done. Remove from pans; cool on wire rack.

Makes 24 buns

English Bath Buns

1¼ cups water

2 tablespoons vegetable oil

2 tablespoons honey

1½ teaspoons salt

2¾ cups all-purpose flour

¾ cup rye flour

½ cup whole bran cereal

2 teaspoons active dry yeast

¼ cup milk

Bran and Honey Rye Breadsticks

1. Measuring carefully, place all ingredients except milk in bread machine pan in order specified by owner's manual. Program dough cycle setting; press start. Grease large baking sheets; set aside.

2. When cycle is complete, remove dough to lightly floured surface. If necessary, knead in additional all-purpose flour to make dough easy to handle. Divide dough into 24 equal pieces. Shape each dough piece into 8-inch rope. Place 2 inches apart on prepared baking sheets. Cover with clean towel; let rise in warm, draft-free place 45 minutes or until doubled in size.

3. Preheat oven to 400°F. Brush breadsticks with milk. Bake 18 to 20 minutes or until golden brown. Remove from baking sheets; cool on wire racks.   *Makes 24 breadsticks*

2 teaspoons sugar

1½ teaspoons active dry yeast

¾ cup warm water (110° to 115°F)

2 tablespoons finely chopped sun-dried tomatoes

1 tablespoon minced basil

1 teaspoon dried basil

1 tablespoon olive oil

½ teaspoon minced garlic

¼ teaspoon salt

1¾ cups bread flour

¼ cup cornmeal

Nonstick cooking spray

1 grilled bell pepper*

¼ teaspoon coarse salt

*Grill bell pepper halves skin-side down on covered grill over medium to hot coals 15 to 25 minutes or until skin is charred, without turning. Remove from grill and place in plastic bag until cool enough to handle, about 10 minutes. Remove skin with paring knife and discard.

Smoked Focaccia

1. Sprinkle sugar and yeast over warm water; stir until yeast is dissolved. Let stand 5 to 10 minutes or until bubbly. Stir in tomatoes, basil, oil, garlic and salt. Add flour, about ½ cup at a time, stirring until dough begins to pull away from side of bowl and forms a ball; stir in cornmeal.

2. Turn out dough onto lightly floured surface; flatten slightly. Knead gently about 5 minutes or until smooth and elastic, adding additional flour to prevent sticking, if necessary. Place dough in large bowl sprayed with nonstick cooking spray and turn dough so all sides are coated. Let rise, covered, in warm place about 1 hour or until doubled in bulk. (Dough may be refrigerated overnight.)

3. Punch down dough; turn onto lightly floured surface and knead 1 minute. Divide dough in half; press each half into a 9×7-inch rectangle on large sheet of foil sprayed with cooking spray. Fold edges of foil to form "pan." Dimple surfaces of dough using fingertips; spray tops with cooking spray. Cut bell pepper into strips and arrange on focaccia; sprinkle with coarse salt. Let rise, covered, 30 minutes.

4. Grill focaccia on covered grill over medium coals 8 to 12 minutes or until they sound hollow when tapped, keeping on foil "pans." Check bottoms of focaccia after about 6 minutes; move to upper grill rack or over indirect heat to finish if browning too quickly. *Makes 6 servings*

367

HEARTY *soups & stews*

Crusty Water Rolls

$^1/_4$ to $^1/_2$ cup warm water (105° to 115°F)

1 package ($^1/_4$ ounce) active dry yeast

1 teaspoon sugar

$^3/_4$ teaspoon salt

2 large egg whites

2$^1/_4$ cups all-purpose flour

2 tablespoons vegetable oil

Cornmeal

Cold water

Combine $^1/_4$ cup water, yeast, sugar and salt. Stir to dissolve yeast; let stand until bubbly, about 5 minutes. Blend in egg whites.

Fit processor with steel blade. Measure flour and oil into work bowl. Process until mixed, about 10 seconds. Turn processor on and very slowly drizzle the yeast mixture through feed tube. Process until blended, about 10 seconds. Turn on processor and very slowly drizzle in just enough remaining water so dough forms a ball that cleans sides of bowl. Process until ball turns around bowl about 25 times. Turn off processor; let dough stand 1 to 2 minutes. Turn on processor; gradually drizzle in enough remaining water to make dough soft and smooth but not sticky. Process until dough turns around bowl about 15 times.

Turn dough onto lightly floured surface. Shape into ball; place in lightly greased bowl, turning to grease all sides. Cover loosely with plastic wrap; let stand in warm place (85°F) until doubled, about 1 hour. Punch down dough. Cover; let rest 10 minutes. Divide dough into 9 equal pieces. Shape each into a smooth ball by gently pulling top surface to underside; pinch bottom to seal. Dip bottom side in cornmeal; place on greased cookie sheet about 1$^1/_2$ inches apart. Cover loosely with plastic wrap; let stand in warm place until doubled, about 1 hour.

Place shallow pan of water on bottom rack of oven. Heat oven to 400°F. Brush rolls with cold water. Bake until golden, 15 to 18 minutes. Brush or spray rolls with cold water once or twice during baking, for crisper crusts. Remove rolls immediately from cookie sheet; cool on wire rack. *Makes 9 rolls*

Clockwise from top right: **Crusty Water Rolls,**
Easy Crescents *(page 370)*, **Cloverleaf Rolls** *(page 371)*

Easy Crescents

1 cup warm water (105° to 115°F)

1 package (¼ ounce) active dry yeast

1 can (5⅓ ounces) evaporated milk

⅓ cup sugar

2 large eggs, divided

1½ teaspoons salt

5½ cups all-purpose flour, divided

¼ cup butter or margarine, melted and cooled

1 cup cold butter or margarine, cut into ¼-inch-thick slices

1 tablespoon cold water

Combine warm water and yeast in 1-quart bowl. Stir to dissolve yeast. Add evaporated milk, sugar, 1 egg, salt and 1 cup flour. Beat mixture with whisk to make a smooth batter. Blend in melted butter. Reserve. Fit processor with steel blade. Measure 3 cups of the remaining flour and cold butter slices into the work bowl. Process on/off 15 to 20 times until butter is in pieces no larger than kidney beans. Transfer mixture to large mixing bowl. Stir in remaining 1½ cups flour.

Pour yeast-milk mixture over flour mixture. Stir with wooden spoon or rubber spatula just until all flour is moistened. Cover tightly and refrigerate until thoroughly chilled, at least 4 hours or up to 3 days. Turn dough onto lightly floured surface. Knead about 6 times. Divide dough into 4 equal parts. Shape 1 part at a time, keeping others in refrigerator.

Roll each part on well floured surface into a circle about 17 inches in diameter. Cut into 8 equal pie-shaped wedges. Roll up each wedge starting at wide end and rolling towards point. Place on ungreased cookie sheets about 1½ inches apart. Curve ends of each roll to form crescent shapes.

Cover loosely with plastic wrap and let stand in warm place (85°F) until doubled, 1 to 1½ hours. Heat oven to 325°F. Beat remaining egg and cold water with a fork. Brush mixture over each roll. Bake until golden, 20 to 25 minutes. Remove immediately from cookie sheets to wire rack. Serve warm.

Makes 32 crescents

Cloverleaf Rolls

³/₄ to 1 cup warm water (105° to
115°F), divided

1 package (¹/₄ ounce) active
dry yeast

2 teaspoons sugar

2³/₄ cups all-purpose flour

2 tablespoons vegetable oil

1 teaspoon salt

Combine ¼ cup of the water, yeast and sugar. Stir to dissolve yeast and let stand until bubbly, about 5 minutes. Fit processor with steel blade. Measure flour, oil and salt into work bowl. Process until mixed, about 15 seconds. Add yeast mixture; process until blended, about 10 seconds.

Turn on processor and very slowly drizzle just enough remaining water through feed tube so dough forms a ball that cleans sides of the bowl. Process until ball turns around bowl about 25 times. Turn off processor and let dough stand 1 to 2 minutes.

Turn on processor and gradually drizzle in enough remaining water to make dough soft, smooth and satiny but not sticky. Process until dough turns around bowl about 15 times. Turn dough onto lightly floured surface. Shape into ball and place in lightly greased bowl, turning to grease all sides. Cover with plastic wrap. Let stand in warm place (85°F) until almost doubled, about 30 minutes.

Divide dough into 12 equal parts. Divide each part into 3 pieces. Shape each into a smooth ball by gently pulling top surface to underside. Pinch bottom to seal. Place 3 balls in each of 12 greased muffin cups. Cover loosely with plastic wrap and let stand in warm place until doubled, 50 to 60 minutes. Heat oven to 375°F. Bake until golden, 15 to 20 minutes. Remove rolls immediately from muffin cups. Serve warm or cool on wire rack.

Makes 1 dozen rolls

371

HEARTY soups & stews

Original Ranch® Oyster Crackers

1   box (16 ounces) oyster crackers

¼   cup vegetable oil

1   packet (1 ounce) HIDDEN
      VALLEY® Original Ranch®
      Salad Dressing & Recipe Mix

Place crackers in a gallon-size Glad Zipper Storage Bag. Pour oil over crackers; seal bag and toss to coat. Add salad dressing & recipe mix; seal bag and toss again until coated. Bake on ungreased baking sheet at 250°F. for 15 to 20 minutes or until crackers are golden brown.

Makes 8 cups

French Twist Potato Bread

1   large COLORADO russet variety potato, peeled and cut up

5½   to 6 cups bread flour or all-purpose flour, divided

2   packages active dry yeast

1   teaspoon salt

1   slightly beaten egg white

1   teaspoon coarse-grained (Kosher) salt

1   teaspoon coarsely ground black pepper

    Cornmeal

In saucepan combine potato and 1 cup water. Bring to a boil; reduce heat. Cover and simmer about 15 minutes or until potato is very tender. Mash potato in liquid. Add additional water to make 2 cups. Cool liquid mixture to 120° to 130°F.

In large mixing bowl combine 1½ cups flour, yeast, 1 teaspoon salt and warm potato mixture. Beat on low speed to mix well; then beat on high speed 3 minutes, scraping sides of bowl. Stir in as much of remaining flour as possible with spoon. Turn out onto floured surface and knead 8 to 10 minutes or until smooth and elastic. Place in greased bowl; let rise in warm place until doubled, about 1 hour.

Combine egg white and 1 tablespoon water; set aside. Punch down dough. Turn out onto floured surface; cut into 4 pieces and let rest 5 minutes. Roll each piece into 12- to 14-inch rope. Brush ropes lightly with egg white mixture; sprinkle lightly with coarse salt and pepper. For each loaf, twist 2 ropes together to form 1 loaf. Place loaves on greased and cornmeal-coated baking sheets. Let rise in warm place until nearly doubled, about 35 to 40 minutes. Bake in 375°F oven 35 to 40 minutes. Brush loaves with remaining egg white about half way through baking time. Cool on wire rack.

Makes 2 loaves

Favorite recipe from **Colorado Potato Administrative Committee**

373

HEARTY *soups & stews*

HEARTY soups & stews

Soft Pretzels

1   cup milk

¹/₃   cup butter, softened

1   teaspoon garlic salt

3   cups all-purpose flour

2   tablespoons sugar

1   teaspoon baking powder

1¹/₂   teaspoons active dry yeast

2   tablespoons baking soda

Coarse salt, sesame seeds or poppy seeds for toppings

1. Measuring carefully, place all ingredients except baking soda and toppings in bread machine pan in order specified by owner's manual. Program dough cycle setting; press start. Grease baking sheets; set aside.

2. When cycle is complete, remove dough to lightly floured surface. If necessary, knead in additional all-purpose flour to make dough easy to handle. Divide dough into 18 equal pieces. Roll each piece into 22-inch-long rope on lightly oiled surface. Form rope into "U" shape. About 2 inches from each end, cross dough. Cross second time. Fold loose ends up to rounded part of "U" and press ends to seal. Turn pretzels over so that ends are on underside, and reshape if necessary. Cover with clean towel; let rest 20 minutes.

3. Preheat oven to 375°F. Fill large Dutch oven ¾ full with water. Bring to a boil over high heat. Add baking soda. Carefully drop pretzels, 3 at a time, into boiling water for 10 seconds. Remove with slotted spoon. Place on prepared baking sheets. Sprinkle with coarse salt, sesame seeds or poppy seeds. Bake 15 to 20 minutes or until golden brown. Remove from baking sheets; cool on wire racks.

Makes 18 large pretzels

Southwestern Biscuits

2¼ cups all-purpose flour

2 tablespoons granulated sugar

1 tablespoon baking powder

½ teaspoon salt (optional)

3 tablespoons butter or margarine, softened

1 egg

1 cup (8-ounce can) cream-style corn

½ cup (4-ounce can) ORTEGA® Diced Green Chiles

1 tablespoon chopped fresh cilantro (optional)

PREHEAT oven to 400°F.

COMBINE flour, sugar and baking powder in large bowl. Add butter; cut in with pastry blender or two knives until mixture resembles coarse crumbs.

STIR in egg, corn, chiles and cilantro, if desired; combine just until mixture holds together. Knead dough 10 times on well-floured surface. Pat dough into ¾-inch thickness. Cut into 3-inch biscuits. Place on greased baking sheets.

BAKE for 20 to 25 minutes or until wooden pick inserted in center comes out clean. Cool on baking sheets for 5 minutes; remove to wire racks to cool completely.

Makes 8 biscuits

375

HEARTY soups & stews

The publisher would like to thank the companies and organizations listed below for the use of their recipes and photographs in this publication.

American Lamb Council

Birds Eye®

Bob Evans®

Butterball® Turkey Company

California Wild Rice Advisory Board

Colorado Potato Administrative Committee

ConAgra Grocery Products Company

Del Monte Corporation

Delmarva Poultry Industry, Inc.

Filippo Berio® Olive Oil

Fleischmann's® Yeast

Florida Department of Agriculture and Consumer Services, Bureau of Seafood and Aquaculture

Florida Tomato Committee

The Golden Grain Company®

Guiltless Gourmet®

Hebrew National®

The Hidden Valley® Food Products Company

Hillshire Farm®

Hormel Foods, LLC

Idaho Potato Commission

Kikkoman International Inc.

Kraft Foods Holdings

Lawry's® Foods, Inc.

McIlhenny Company (TABASCO® brand Pepper Sauce)

Mrs. T's Pierogies

Mushroom Council

National Honey Board

National Pork Board

Nestlé USA

Norseland, Inc. Lucini Italia Co.

North Dakota Wheat Commission

The Procter & Gamble Company

Reckitt Benckiser

RED STAR® Yeast, a product of Lasaffre Yeast Corporation

Riviana Foods Inc.

Sargento® Foods Inc.

StarKist® Seafood Company

The Sugar Association, Inc.

Uncle Ben's Inc.

Unilever Bestfoods North America

USA Rice Federation

Wisconsin Milk Marketing Board

Index

377

HEARTY soups & stews

POZOLE BISQUE CHOWDER CHILI BOUILLABAISSE GUMBO PISTOU CIOPPIN

Index

379

HEARTY *soups & stews*

OZOLE BISQUE CHOWDER CHILI BOUILLABAISSE GUMBO PISTOU CIOPPINO

POZOLE BISQUE CHOWDER CHILI BOUILLABAISSE GUMBO PISTOU CIOPPIN

Index

383

HEARTY soups & stews

METRIC CONVERSION CHART

VOLUME MEASUREMENTS (dry)

$1/8$ teaspoon = 0.5 mL
$1/4$ teaspoon = 1 mL
$1/2$ teaspoon = 2 mL
$3/4$ teaspoon = 4 mL
1 teaspoon = 5 mL
1 tablespoon = 15 mL
2 tablespoons = 30 mL
$1/4$ cup = 60 mL
$1/3$ cup = 75 mL
$1/2$ cup = 125 mL
$2/3$ cup = 150 mL
$3/4$ cup = 175 mL
1 cup = 250 mL
2 cups = 1 pint = 500 mL
3 cups = 750 mL
4 cups = 1 quart = 1 L

VOLUME MEASUREMENTS (fluid)

1 fluid ounce (2 tablespoons) = 30 mL
4 fluid ounces ($1/2$ cup) = 125 mL
8 fluid ounces (1 cup) = 250 mL
12 fluid ounces ($1 1/2$ cups) = 375 mL
16 fluid ounces (2 cups) = 500 mL

WEIGHTS (mass)

$1/2$ ounce = 15 g
1 ounce = 30 g
3 ounces = 90 g
4 ounces = 120 g
8 ounces = 225 g
10 ounces = 285 g
12 ounces = 360 g
16 ounces = 1 pound = 450 g

DIMENSIONS

$1/16$ inch = 2 mm
$1/8$ inch = 3 mm
$1/4$ inch = 6 mm
$1/2$ inch = 1.5 cm
$3/4$ inch = 2 cm
1 inch = 2.5 cm

OVEN TEMPERATURES

250°F = 120°C
275°F = 140°C
300°F = 150°C
325°F = 160°C
350°F = 180°C
375°F = 190°C
400°F = 200°C
425°F = 220°C
450°F = 230°C

BAKING PAN SIZES

Utensil	Size in Inches/Quarts	Metric Volume	Size in Centimeters
Baking or Cake Pan (square or rectangular)	8×8×2	2 L	20×20×5
	9×9×2	2.5 L	23×23×5
	12×8×2	3 L	30×20×5
	13×9×2	3.5 L	33×23×5
Loaf Pan	8×4×3	1.5 L	20×10×7
	9×5×3	2 L	23×13×7
Round Layer Cake Pan	8×1½	1.2 L	20×4
	9×1½	1.5 L	23×4
Pie Plate	8×1¼	750 mL	20×3
	9×1¼	1 L	23×3
Baking Dish or Casserole	1 quart	1 L	—
	1½ quart	1.5 L	—
	2 quart	2 L	—

GUMBO PISTOU CIOPPINO POZOLE B

POZOLE BISQUE CHOWDER CHILI BO

CHOWDER CHILI BOUILLABAISSE GUM

BOUILLABAISSE GUMBO PISTOU CIOP

PISTOU CIOPPINO POZOLE BISQUE C

BISQUE CHOWDER CHILI BOUILLABAI

CHILI BOUILLABAISSE GUMBO PISTOU

GUMBO PISTOU CIOPPINO POZOLE B

POZOLE BISQUE CHOWDER CHILI BO

CHOWDER CHILI BOUILLABAISSE GUM